WHY WE ARGUE AND HOW TO STOP

A Therapist's Guide to Navigating Disagreements, Managing Emotions, and Creating Healthier Relationships

Jerry Manney

TCK PUBLISHING.COM

ISBN:
978-1-63161-175-9

Sign up for Jerry Manney's newsletter at
www.jerrymanney.com/newsletter

Published by TCK Publishing
www.TCKpublishing.com

Get discounts and special deals on our best selling books at
www.TCKpublishing.com/bookdeals

Check out additional discounts for bulk orders at
www.TCKpublishing.com/bulk-book-orders

Table of Contents

INTRODUCTION

What This Book Can Do for You

Regardless of what we argue about or why we argue, it boils down to this: we're trying to make someone think or act the way we want them to, and we're met with the usual result—pushback. In this book, I will show you how to catch yourself before you get caught up in a troublesome debate, and how not to invite yourself or others to arguments. I'll give you specific techniques with examples you can use to help others really hear and consider your concerns, whether those people are your loved ones, friends, co-workers, roommates, customer service representatives—even your ex who is the parent of your children. I'll also show you how to manage the emotions that often invite you and others to heated and unproductive exchanges.

I won't cover every possible scenario you may encounter in your daily interactions because that's just not practical. Instead, I will give you adapted, scientifically-validated Positive Communication tools and practical strategies that have been shown to work for many people in many different (and difficult) situations. You will have opportunities to customize the practice exercises throughout this book so that they address your particular concerns before you use those strategies in real-life situations.

I've drawn upon my extensive work as a counselor, the research of other experts in various fields, and my own personal experience as a long-time member of a 12-step program for families of alcoholics to create this comprehensive resource that will help you manage the strong emotions that are both the great blessings and the great challenges of being human. This will enable you to successfully use the communication skills you'll learn here with people you are close to, people you are not close to, and especially those you don't ever want to get close to, but who seem to invite you to arguments anyway.

How to Use This Book

Think of this book as a toolkit, and your role is to select the right tool for the right occasion. How many of us have hastily reached for a screwdriver and instead picked up a butter knife? The butter knife may be a useful tool but, not being designed for the matter at hand, it will slip out of the screw head and scratch the surface of whatever you're working on, or worse, jab you in your other hand. Using the wrong tool for the job can get you (and others) unnecessarily hurt.

I do not suggest reading this entire book in one sitting. Instead, take some time to digest the information as you go along.

This book is not intended to be a substitute for professional assessment or counseling, but it can be a valuable steppingstone to additional help and a supplement to counseling. Chapter Ten, *What To Do When You Need More Help*, will explore common issues that often require special assistance, as well as how you can find the right professional for any difficult situation or relationship.

Where I have borrowed from the wisdom of others, I have provided sources to allow you the opportunity for some further reading. Statements in this book that are in quotation marks and without a reference are, to the best of my knowledge, from anonymous sources. Some have been around a long time, and many have been popularized by members of self-help programs. The thoughts and comments described throughout this book probably have, in a calmer moment, crossed many people's minds.

I have designed this book to be as practical as possible

so you can build upon your existing strengths and identify the stuck points and common communication traps that may trigger or escalate arguments. You can also find additional tools and resources at www.jerrymanney.com/resources.

As you learn and practice new communication and coping tools, you will continue to acquire more effective communication and relational skills. You'll feel more self-confident, knowing that you can handle even the toughest situations (and people) better than you ever have before. And, you'll find that the people around you trust you more and are more willing to open up, be vulnerable, and work with you more amicably.

Prepare for Success

Throughout this book, I'll encourage you to write, in a separate journal or on an electronic device, your thoughts, emotions, and prior attempts at communicating. These requests will be flagged by the symbol ✐.

I'll also ask you to practice specific communication techniques in writing *before* you use them with others, and I encourage you to take notes, recording your thoughts and questions whenever something important comes to mind. I urge you to take time to record and organize the main areas or goals you want to focus on, as well as specific tools and ideas you want to continue using to work toward your goals.

According to noted research psychologist Robert J. Meyers:

> "If there is one overriding 'fact' in the world of behavior change, it is that people who record important information about their lives are people most likely to succeed in making important changes in their lives."[1]

Journaling is important because memory is unreliable. A journal will give you a tangible, useful tool for making meaningful changes in your life. I learned a long time ago that one of the key characteristics of a knowledgeable and successful person is not how much they can remember, but whether they have a method or system for accessing important and relevant information when they need it. It's a lot easier to make positive changes in your life when you have the information you need, time to reflect, and a system for focusing on what you want. Journaling is one of the best systems I've ever discovered to help you get just that.

Venting your feelings on paper or on a screen can also be a healthy and helpful way to release strong emotions, and to gain new insights into your concerns so you can more clearly understand any underlying issues and find a path forward. You can do this during your free time, or even at night when your emotions or thoughts may keep you awake.

Tips for Journaling

When writing or typing in your journal, don't be concerned about neatness, spelling, or grammar. This will free your mind to write or type as quickly as you need to so you can focus on recording your thoughts, feelings, questions, and ideas—anything that comes to mind, even if it does not seem to make a lot of sense in the moment. I also encourage the frequent use of abbreviations, even making up your own, provided you'll understand them later. Once you've finished recording your thoughts, reread what you have written and clarify anything that seems unclear.

Try to take an electronic device or small notepad with you wherever you go, so that when an idea or question pops into your head, you can quickly record it. If you find yourself replaying heated or otherwise unsatisfactory conversations in your head, try writing down your thoughts instead of just thinking about it. Jot down any questions or ideas you have about discussions that didn't go as well as you would have liked so you don't have to rely solely on your memory when reflecting on a painful or uncomfortable conversation. Memory will let you down, but the more details you can record along the way, the more insights you are likely to gain.

You can write in your journal for however long is necessary—until you feel somewhat relieved or tired, or for only a few minutes if you have a particular thought or idea. Noting ideas or concerns in the moment, while they are still fresh in your mind, will also enable you to process them in more depth, and at a later time and place that may be more convenient.

By dating each entry, you can also review your progress over time, which can provide invaluable support and encouragement. Reviewing recorded information can help you gain more detailed insights, instead of relying solely on your long-term memory. Keeping an electronic journal with a protected password can afford an additional feeling of confidentiality.

If you don't already have a journal, make a note to purchase one or set up an electronic one by a specific date. In the meantime, locate a writing pad or even some scrap paper to record insights, goals, and questions as they come to you.

✐ Moving Forward

Take a few moments to begin journaling right now. Briefly record the main goals you want to focus on while working through this book.

- What skills would you like to learn?

- Which of your relationships would you like to focus on and improve?

CHAPTER ONE

Why Do We Argue?

We've all been there, probably more times than we care to remember: You overreacted to your partner's annoying behavior, a parent who managed to push your buttons, or a roommate's misplaced shoes that you ended up tripping over. Perhaps you avoided talking about an issue until it built up and boiled over, or you had a stressful day and some minor thing made you lose your temper. Other times, conversations start out innocently enough and then suddenly speed up faster than a car without brakes going down a steep hill. You tell yourself to bite your tongue, or that it's not worth getting upset over—but you still get really ticked off! If it's any consolation, you are not alone; yes, it even happened on occasion to Mahatma Gandhi and Mother Theresa.

Why do we argue? Some will say it is most often about money, including which purchases to make or which bills to pay first. Others will say it is about housework, dirty dishes, soiled clothes on the floor, or strong disagreements over political, religious, or personal issues. But those things are *what* people argue about, not *why* they argue.

 ## Why We Actually Argue

So, why do we actually argue? Here are some possibilities:

- You take a disagreement personally—that is, you infer that the other person not only thinks your opinion is wrong, but that *you* are wrong.

- You think that if you disagree with someone, one of

you must be right and the other must be wrong.

- You believe you are right, the other person is wrong, and that you can change their mind.
- You want someone to change, they want you to change, and neither of you feel like the other is listening or taking responsibility for the conflict.
- By arguing, you hope to convince yourself that your opinion is correct.
- You argue as a form of competition. You tell yourself, "They are not going to win this time."
- If you feel criticized or otherwise provoked, you fight back.
- You think that if you repeat yourself enough times, or say it differently or more loudly, they will finally get it.
- You lose your temper and become defensive.
- You argue to wear the other person down.
- You feel hurt and want to retaliate.
- Sometimes you simply enjoy arguing.
- You want to prove a point.
- You blame someone else when something doesn't go your way.
- You don't know what else to do.
- You shut down when confronted.
- You know what is best for your child.
- You argue because you are a human being with emotions that can sometimes overwhelm you.
- Your argument is a statement or opinion backed by rational, logical thought.

Do you notice a common theme here? We often argue because we're trying to change the thinking or behavior of someone else.

To get a better understanding of why people don't always respond the way you'd like them to, try thinking about things from a different perspective. Imagine you are in their shoes, listening to what you said to them. How do you usually react when you feel someone is trying to change the way you think or act? How would that make you feel? What would you say to them? How likely would you be to treat them as kindly and compassionately as possible?

But it's not the same, you say? You had the other person's best interests in mind? They started the argument? You work hard at being a good partner, parent, daughter, son, or coworker? You try harder? They just don't care? While there may be some truth in your reactions, the deeper truth is that all of us want to feel like we're being listened to, respected, and acknowledged, even if we don't always make constructive decisions or treat others as well as we'd like to.

Some situations in life will trigger intense emotions for you, while others won't even phase you at all. The more emotional you feel about an issue, the more likely you are to get into a heated argument over it. If a complete stranger told you the earth is flat, how likely is it that you would get into an argument? Most people would completely ignore the remark and see no point in responding.

It's hard to check your emotions when you feel strongly about a subject, but if you continue the habit of getting defensive and justifying your reactions, you might wind up arguing about why you argue so much, and maybe even forget what started the current argument. If you find yourself in a situation where you don't even know why you're arguing, the best thing you can do is stop, take a moment to reflect, and consider things from the other person's perspective.

Identifying Your Argument Patterns

Now that you understand some basics about why people argue in general, it's time to figure out why *you* argue. We're going to identify your specific arguing patterns to help you cultivate more awareness of which situations upset you and make you more likely to get into heated arguments. Then, once you know what your patterns are, we'll begin the process of changing them one step at a time.

You're about to begin the *Why do I argue?* self-questionnaire. In your journal, complete each sentence stem from the questionnaire. Try to be as specific as you can. For example, instead of making the broad statement "I wish to improve my communication with loved ones," write the name of the person, their relationship to you, and what precisely you want to change. Communicating specifics is a great skill that will help you avoid arguments that start from misunderstandings. The more clarity you bring to this exercise, the sooner you'll be able to change the patterns of behavior that keep you stuck in heated arguments.

If you're unable to think of a specific response while completing the questionnaire, enter what you can for the time being. Then, come back to those responses the next day and see if you can find more clarity.

You can return to this and any of the other exercises and activities later to review what you previously noted, record additional insights, or give yourself the praise you deserve for making progress.

Here are some examples to help you get started.

Example 1:

If I take a disagreement personally, I tend to infer that the other person not only thinks my opinion is wrong, but that *I* am wrong. I often do this with my boyfriend and my mother, and then I get very defensive and disagree with their feedback instead of listening to them and honestly considering what they're saying. I would like to be able to catch myself before I react, and I would like to be able to listen to what they have to say and try to understand them, even when I find what they're saying to be upsetting.

Example 2:

Some of the things other people say can make me so angry. For example, when my older brother, Jack, starts telling me what I should or shouldn't do, I start yelling, and then he criticizes me even more. It's been that way since we were kids. I feel guilty when I yell and lose my cool, and I'd like to find a better way to respond. I want to remind myself to use a time-out before things escalate. I would also like to tell Jack how I feel when he gives me unsolicited advice, and I want to ask him to stop trying to tell me what I should do unless I ask for his advice.

✎ *Why do I argue?* Self-Questionnaire

This self-questionnaire is available to download or print from my website, www.jerrymanney.com/resources. Please note that you do not have to answer every question.

1. If I take a disagreement personally, I am likely to infer that the other person not only thinks my opinion is wrong, but that *I* am wrong. I tend to do this with [name of the person and their relationship to you]. I would like to [insert your goal for improvement].

2. Some of the things other people say can make me so angry. When [name, relationship] says [insert

comment], I often [insert observation]. I would like to [insert your goal for improvement].

3. I thought if I disagreed with someone that one of us had to be right and the other had to be wrong. I tend to do this with [name, relationship]. This can result in [outcome]. I would like to [insert your goal for improvement].

4. When I believe I'm right and the other person is wrong, I think I can change their mind, and so I'll often [insert your pattern]. I tend to do this with [name, relationship]. I would like to [insert your goal].

5. By arguing, I can sometimes convince myself that my opinion is right. This often makes me feel [insert your comment]. I tend to do this with [name, relationship]. I would like to [insert your goal].

6. Sometimes arguing becomes a form of competition for me. I think, "They are not going to win this time," and then I [insert your pattern]. I tend to do this with [name, relationship]. I would like to [insert your goal].

7. When I feel criticized or otherwise provoked, I fight back. Then, I [insert your pattern]. I tend to do this with [name, relationship]. I would like to [insert your goal].

8. Sometimes, I think that if I repeat myself enough times, say it differently, or say it louder, they will finally get it. This is more likely to happen with [name, relationship]. This usually results in [insert usual outcome]. I would like to [insert your goal].

9. Sometimes, when I lose my temper, I can become

defensive and then [insert your pattern]. I tend to do this with [name, relationship]. I would like to [insert your goal].

10. When I feel hurt, I may feel like retaliating. Then I [insert your pattern]. I tend to do this with [name, relationship]. I would like to [insert your goal].

11. Sometimes, I like to argue. Later, I [insert your pattern]. I tend to do this with [name, relationship]. I would like to [insert your goal].

12. Sometimes, I will argue to prove a point. This usually results in [insert usual outcome]. I tend to do this with [name, relationship]. I would like to [insert your goal].

13. At times, I blame others when something doesn't go my way. Later I feel [insert your comment]. I tend to do this with [name, relationship]. I would like to [insert your goal].

14. Sometimes, I argue because I don't know what else to do at that moment. Afterward, I feel [insert your comment]. I tend to do this with [name, relationship]. I would like to [insert your goal].

15. I sometimes shut down when confronted. This usually results in [insert usual outcome]. I tend to do this with [name, relationship]. I would like to [insert your goal].

16. I don't know why I keep getting into certain arguments. This is more likely to happen with [name, relationship]. I would like to [insert your goal].

17. At times, I find myself thinking, "But if they would just listen to reason . . .". This usually happens

with [name, relationship], and then [insert usual outcome]. I would like to [insert your goal].

18. At times, I find myself thinking, "But I know what is best for [name, relationship]." Later, [insert usual outcome]. I would like to [insert your goal].

19. At times, I find myself thinking that [name, relationship] wants me to change, but *they* are not willing to change, and we continue to butt heads! Then I feel [insert your comment]. I would like to [insert your goal].

20. An argument can also be a statement or opinion backed by rational, logical thought. This applies to me when [insert your comment]. When this happens, I feel [insert your comment].

21. Other examples of why I argue: [insert your comments and observations].

In Chapter Five, *Get Your Concerns Really Heard,* you will be able to use these responses and other examples as a starting point for Positive Communication. These techniques will help you get your concerns really heard in a more open-minded and less defensive manner.

I would love to tell you that I practice in my daily life all that I have learned from two college degrees, many years of professional experience, and continued training and readings—but I am human. Sitting in the counselor's chair, where I focus on helping others with their struggles, is far easier than dealing with my own issues. My professional and personal experiences have taught me that it's not about attaining perfection; instead, it's about the process—the more you learn and try, the better you get, and that sense of progress will help you get more of what you want in life and in your relationships.

There are things you can do to prevent matters from getting worse, which we'll discuss in the very next chapter, *Put the Brakes on Heated Arguments*.

✎ Moving Forward

- What is one thing that you have learned about yourself or your patterns by completing the "Why do I argue?" Self-Questionnaire?

- Record one or two specific goals you want to achieve using the lessons and insights from this chapter.

CHAPTER TWO

Put the Brakes on Heated Arguments

Psychotherapists and self-help authors typically encourage people to talk more to each other about their feelings and concerns. There are times, however, when it is better not to continue talking, and instead call a "time-out" to prevent an escalation of anger, frustration, and hurt feelings, which can trigger and fuel heated arguments, resulting in more anger, frustration, and hurt feelings.

At a calm (or relatively calm) moment, discussing the seven guidelines for time-outs (which you'll find below) can put the brakes on heated arguments so you can slow down and regain your focus. When you find yourself in an argument and you're not sure what to do, remember to "de-escalate before it's too late."

Seven Points About Time-Outs

1. Anyone (spouse, partner, teenagers, children, adults, coworkers, etc.) can call a time-out if they feel that they are about to lose their temper or objectivity and perhaps say things they may later regret. Someone may also call a time-out if they think the other person is losing or is about to lose their temper.

2. Clarify that calling a time-out is not disrespectful (provided you don't overuse it), and that you will attempt to discuss the issue constructively within a reasonable timeframe. A time-out is about

respecting yourself and each other, and recognizing that when emotions begin to flare, taking time to regain your composure can help strengthen and nurture the relationship, whether it be with a family member, friend, or coworker.

3.   A brief statement such as, "Let's talk about this later (or after lunch or tomorrow)" can help reassure the other person that you're serious about resuming the discussion. However, when your emotions are escalating, any attempts to explain why you don't want to continue talking will likely further the argument.

4.   When someone calls a time-out, the other person does not have to agree with the timing of the time-out.

5.   Once a time-out is called, the parties need to separate themselves physically in a manner that is as respectful as possible. This may seem awkward at first, but in my experience, most people find this separation very helpful.

6.   Any brief and respectful phrase can be used in place of the term "time-out" to communicate similar intentions. Ideally, try to agree on the words you'd like each other to use when talking about these guidelines. A "reasonable time" for a time-out is flexible; it could be minutes or hours, or perhaps a few days. As soon as everyone involved has been able to calm down and think more clearly, reconvene to discuss the situation.

7.   While there is no perfect time to plan or reschedule a discussion, there are times to avoid engaging in difficult discussions. You probably know when these

are: immediately after waking up in the morning, within the first few minutes of a person arriving home, while one person is driving or engaged in a potentially mentally challenging activity, and shortly before mealtime or bedtime.

🖉 What other times and places do you think would be best avoided when it comes to important or sensitive discussions? What times and places could help the conversation unfold more calmly and constructively? Take out your journal and create these two lists.

Getting in the Habit of Using Time-Outs

As with any new tool, it may take some time to remember that time-outs are available when you need them. But as you continue to gain insights and experience, you will learn to anticipate factors that are likely to trigger an argument. Over time, as trust in this process develops, time-outs may occur without someone having to announce "time-out." Instead, there will be mutual recognition that a cooling-off period is in each person's best interests. Plan where you can go during a time-out for some privacy—perhaps your bedroom or outdoors, if weather permits.

After everyone has achieved a mutual cooling-off (at least for the most part), suggest a time to resume the discussion and ask if that would be all right with the other person. If this appears to lead to another argument or resumption of the previous one, say something like, "Maybe we need some more time to let things cool down." Certain issues may benefit from a longer cooling-off period and additional preparation. In Chapter Eight, you will develop specific step-by-step strategies to help you deal with more challenging concerns.

While some issues need more time, delaying a follow-up conversation more than several days may lead you to think it's not important anymore, or to put off or avoid the issue altogether. When this happens, concerns can build up and catch you off-guard the next time something triggers a resumption of the same argument or adds fuel to a new disagreement. Be sure that you do address the issue at some point and don't just sweep it under the rug.

You can also use the period of a time-out to write down your thoughts about what triggered this particular argument. Look at the parts you were in control of, including what you said and how you said it, and how you responded or reacted to the other person's comments. Remember, this is not about who was or who was not at fault; dwelling on that only keeps the argument going inside your head (and perhaps in the pit of your stomach). Rather, it's as an opportunity to take a recent, specific example of interpersonal conflict, gain a clearer, more in-depth picture of your interactions with others, and incorporate one or more of the tools and strategies you think might help you resolve the problem.

Frequently Asked Questions About Using Time-Outs

What do I do if the time-out has no effect?

It's all too easy to get caught in the middle of an argument between family members, friends, acquaintances, and, depending on the topic, even strangers. Remember: the reason for walking away is to avoid engaging in or contributing to an argument that is heating up and becoming counterproductive, or even painful. The more people involved in a heated argument, the more heated it is likely to become.

No matter how close or caring a couple, family, or friendship, each person is an individual and will figure things out at their own pace. Someone needs to be the first to get off the "here we go again, not-so-merry-go-round" of heated, upsetting, hurtful, or counterproductive arguments. By focusing on what you can change—*your response*—instead of reacting to what you cannot change—*how others act*—you are taking two steps forward. First, you will get off the "not-so-merry-go-round" by choosing to no longer contribute to escalating arguments. Second, you'll set a tangible example of constructive change.

During a time-out, the other person may text or call you. Let the call go to voicemail and then listen to it. Unless the call or text concerns an urgent matter, waiting until you have regained your composure before you reply can help prevent the argument from reigniting. If the person continues to text or call, you do not have to read every text or listen to every message. You can also choose to turn off your phone for a brief period. Remind yourself that the purpose of a time-out is to give yourself and the other person enough time to promote more constructive, respectful communication.

Do we both have to agree to the concept of a time-out?

It may take some time for the other person to realize the importance of using time-outs. When you discuss time-outs, focus on presenting them as an idea, rather than trying to make the other person agree to using them. If the other person agrees with you when you first present the information on using time-outs, that's great. If not, allowing them time to think the concept over is a sign of respect, and demonstrates an improvement in your own communication style.

This can also be an opportunity to practice not going to every argument you're invited to. If the other person persistently disagrees with the concept of time-outs, let them know you still plan to try it, and give just a few brief, constructive reasons for your decision. Say something like: "I know I can get off-topic when things get heated;" "I really want to improve our communication, and I think it would be better if we took a break and talked after we've both had a chance to cool off;" or, "I think it would be a good idea if we took a break and continued this conversation later. I'll get back to you as soon as I can to arrange a time."

What if the other person appears to be under the influence of a substance?

Trying to have a discussion with someone whose thinking and judgment are impaired by alcohol or drugs can be as frustrating as trying to talk to someone who speaks a different language. Even if the other person is not staggering or obviously high, alcohol and other mood-altering drugs can affect the brain's limbic system, which controls emotions. Alcohol and other drugs can also affect parts of the brain that influence impulse control, decision-making, short-term memory, and other functions important in interpersonal communication. Postpone the conversation to another time when the opportunity for clear, mutual communication may be more feasible. If the drinking or drug use may be causing or contributing to ongoing arguments or financial problems, health issues, injuries, legal problems, or other concerns, Chapter Ten will clarify when and how to find professional help.

When Time-Outs Don't Work

A time-out may backfire if there is any violence in the relationship. The perpetrator could interpret the pause as a threat, and more violence, such as pushing, shoving, or hitting may result. An aggressor may also make threats to harm you, your children, and/or someone else in the home. If there has been any incidence of grabbing, squeezing, choking, or any other action that causes you pain or fear, *do not suggest a time-out.* Skip the rest of the pages and read the sections *Physical Violence and How to Find Help* in Chapter Ten to learn how to get confidential help and support. Remember, there is hope.

Four Ground Rules for Saner Communication

Having a few healthy boundaries in place can help you better navigate interpersonal conversations, and also make those conversations more productive and enjoyable. Picture how stressful and hazardous driving would be without basic rules of the road, such as keeping to the right (or left), or yielding to oncoming vehicles.

So, to keep your communication sane and productive, here are four ground rules: √

1. Discuss one concern at a time.

2. Only one person speaks at a time.

3. Know the difference between venting with someone and venting at someone.

4. No name-calling.

Let's look at each of these in turn.

Discuss One Concern at a Time

Years ago, I was facilitating a psychoeducational group at an alternative high school and decided to use a visual demonstration to show how difficult it can be to discuss multiple issues at the same time. You can try this exercise at home or your place of employment with either soft-foam balls, rolled-up socks, or similarly soft items.

It works like this:

A volunteer "catcher" stands about eight to ten feet in front of three to five people who line up, side by side, facing the catcher. Decide who will be the initial "thrower." The initial catcher then calls out "one, two, three, throw!" After the word "throw," the first thrower gently lobs one ball or rolled-up sock, underhand, to the catcher in front, aiming for the middle of the catcher's chest or stomach area. (No overhand throws or aiming for the catcher's face!) Most people will find catching the object quite easy. Next, have the same catcher call "one, two, three, throw!" After the word "throw," each of the throwers gently lobs their ball or sock underhand at the same time toward the middle of the catcher's chest or stomach. Now, most catchers will only catch one or even no balls because they're visually distracted by the numerous objects being thrown at them. This is why ocean fish swim in large groups, or "schools": predators are so distracted by all that movement that they can become overwhelmed and perform poorly when trying to catch fish. People also get distracted and perform poorly when attempting to discuss multiple issues at once.

In this activity, each thrower can take a turn being the catcher. Usually, each person thinks they can catch more balls or socks than the others, until they learn that this is much harder than it seems. When I facilitated that school group, the students called upon me to be the catcher after they'd all had a chance. As a former athlete with good hand-eye coordination, I expected to catch two or three of the six balls lobbed my way, despite the degree of difficulty. I wound up catching exactly zero balls—a lesson learned by all.

Discussions are more likely to turn into arguments when multiple concerns get brought into play. Throw in emotion, and those gently lobbed soft balls can escalate into hard balls tossed with reckless abandon. While there may be different concerns that each person thinks are important to discuss, having a few ground rules such as "one ball in the air at a time" or "one concern at a time" acknowledges the importance of each person's concern. This also recognizes that having too many balls in the air—or too many concerns being discussed at once—significantly increases the likelihood that a reasonably calm conversation will soon get out of hand.

Remind the others in a constructive tone: "I hear that you would like to talk about another concern or idea. Can we talk about that in a while when we each agree that we've discussed the present matter enough?"

If additional concerns continue to be raised, it may be necessary to repeat the reminder, either word for word or by rephrasing it: "Remember when we did that soft-ball toss? Can we stick to one ball or concern at a time so that we can give our full attention to it? When we discuss your concern, I will also try to give it my full attention." If the other person appears unable to stick to one concern at a time, a time-out may be needed to prevent emotions from escalating to the point that a constructive discussion is unlikely.

Remember: it takes two or more people to argue; if only ✓ one person wants to argue, an argument does not happen!

Another important part of dealing with one concern at a time is shutting down electronic devices or putting cellphones on mute for the duration of your discussion. More and more research suggests that multitasking overloads the brain, and that we are most efficient when we can focus on a single task.[2]

One Person Speaks at a Time

Interrupting someone is one of the surest ways to escalate a discussion into an argument, which is why the second ground rule is for only one person to speak at a time. Allowing the other person to finish what they are saying helps set the stage for positive and respectful communication. Speaking in turn can also stop the conversation from speeding up too quickly.

If you find yourself having knee-jerk reactions, sticking to one topic at a time can help you think more clearly and say things in a kinder and less confrontational way, ultimately helping you get more of what you really want out of the conversation. It's also important to note that calling for a time-out, even if it involves interrupting someone else, is still preferable to losing your poise and adding fuel to the fire by yelling or becoming defensive.

Vent *with* Someone Instead of *at* Someone

You may have had a particularly frustrating, demanding, and challenging day. It might be as simple as banging your knee hard against a doorway and *BAM!* out comes a loud tirade of comments about anything and everything that has been bothering you for a long time. As human beings, it's not always possible, often to our later regret and remorse, to prevent a blowup or meltdown in which we unleash our frustrations and aggravations out loud. But how can we deal with these strong emotions to regain our composure?

Picture a pressure cooker sitting on a stove. It is designed to cook certain foods more quickly and more economically by trapping heat inside the secured lid. There is a safety valve built into the lid that opens automatically, releasing heat in the form of steam once the pressure reaches a certain level. That's how it's designed to function; putting your hand or, worse, your face, near the escaping steam is a sure way to get badly burned. If the safety valve were to malfunction and not open, you would need to either remove the pot from the stove or turn off the heat to avoid a potential explosion.

Healthy venting is venting *with* someone to release some steam. This means asking the other person, "Do you have a few minutes? I need to tell someone about the lousy day I had," or "Something very upsetting happened earlier today. Can I tell you about it? Would this be a good time?" Asking informs the other person that this is not about them, and gives them the chance to say yes or no. It also gives them the opportunity to say, "Yes. Can you give me a few minutes so I can just finish what I was doing?" It provides the opportunity for them to give you, barring any unforeseen or unavoidable interruptions, their attention and support. Venting *at* someone does not ask for that permission and shows the other person a lack of respect for their time and whatever they might be dealing with at the moment.

No Name-Calling

The childhood rhyme "Sticks and stones may break my bones, but names will never hurt me" was designed to help children deal with verbal assaults, and it can be helpful in that respect. But of course, we all know that words can and do hurt. Adding "no name-calling" to the ground rules for saner communication can also help build a foundation for healthier and more constructive communication.

As you continue to learn more communication techniques and coping skills, you will have considerably more effective alternatives to any less-than-desirable patterns you may have picked up in the past.

Other Ways of Dealing with Tension and Stress

Many people find that some sort of physical activity, such as walking, biking, running, or even performing a household chore can help reduce tension and stress. It might even be enjoyable. Physical activity can help burn up excess adrenaline, release muscular tension, improve circulation, and slow down your thinking. A word of warning: be careful not to over-exert yourself under these circumstances, as you may not be aware of how much adrenaline is pumping through your body. You may become distracted with your thoughts and inattentive to the physical task at hand, which, depending on the activity, could increase the chance of injury. For instance, hopping behind the wheel of a car when you're extremely upset is not a good idea. Your mood may distract you from the multiple tasks necessary to navigate safely.

You may also find it helpful to listen to music. It can take some time to discover which type of music helps with the particular emotion you are experiencing, and which types may make you feel worse. Others may suggest punching a pillow when you're angry, but most professionals recommend against using your fists to release anger. Yelling into a pillow, however, can be a cathartic release.

Some unhealthy ways of dealing with frustrations, tension, and stress are trying to "tough it out" to the point that your physical or emotional health is affected, repeatedly using alcohol or other substances to "take the edge off" a hard day, over-eating, or engaging in any behavior that is not in your best interest.

✎ What are some of the healthy ways you try (or would like to try) to release frustrations, tensions, and stress before they build into potential volcanic-like eruptions?

Apologizing

Often, a brief and heartfelt "I am sorry" will stop an argument in its tracks, especially if done quickly enough.

If that doesn't work, it may not be because you didn't do it effectively. It may simply take a while for the other person to process what you said, as well as their own emotions. Remember, we are not machines, and there's no secret word you can say to instantly end an argument or force someone to let go of their emotions.

By practicing the techniques from this book, you're more likely to feel a sense of progress, confidence, and hope. You're also more likely to gain credibility with others by showing them that you are making real changes in how you interact with them. Apologizing can be a big step in healing the hurts that result from not only an occasional slip of the tongue or even a big blowout argument, but also from an ongoing period of "hurt people hurting each other."

Try not to get stuck in a stubborn contest of who will (or should) apologize first. An apology followed by a 'but' is not a true apology, but rather a justification for your actions.[3] A comment like "I am sorry for yelling, but I was tired from working so late" will have far more credibility when followed by, "and I know that is no excuse to talk to you in that tone of voice."

Whether or not someone accepts your apology is not in your control. You can only control your part, which is making a heartfelt apology when appropriate and redirecting your time and energy into practicing more effective communication.

Ripple Effects

Surely at some point, you've seen a pebble or stone on the shore of a pond and been tempted to toss it into the water—it's such a simple act, and so much fun. Tossing a pebble into a pond creates a ripple effect of concentric circles that expand from the spot where the pebble penetrates the surface of the water. Every positive action you take in changing your communication with others also has a ripple effect. How you interact with others creates a dynamic that continues to grow from the source, just like the concentric circles around the pebble. It changes the dynamic of future interactions, where communication will no longer be the same as it was in the past. You can set in motion positive changes in your communication style that have the distinct potential to influence positive change in those around you.

As you become more skilled at declining invitations to argue, the people you regularly interact with will also be more prone to change. Your practice of respectful, non-confrontational communication will make it more difficult for others to rationalize their own continued use of aggressive, hurtful, or otherwise less constructive behaviors.

When you watch or listen to the news, do you think there just might be a few more people out there who could benefit from the use of more effective communication skills? Positive and respectful communication is contagious. Let's start a positive communication epidemic.

Moving Forward

- Do your arguments typically break any of the four ground rules for saner communicating? How do you think this has affected your communication and relationships with others?

- Which rule do you think you could follow better? Focus on that rule in your interactions this week, then reflect on how you think it's changed your conversations.

CHAPTER THREE

Try Different, Not Harder

Early in my professional career, I spent four years conducting *screening, brief intervention,* and *referral to treatment* in a local general hospital with patients who suffered from alcohol abuse. To improve my ability to help these patients and their families, I also began attending open 12-step meetings. At these meetings, I could identify many psychological and educational principles. However, they appeared to be used in more concise and practical ways than I had been taught in my undergraduate studies in education.

What I could not foresee was that a dozen or so years and an additional graduate degree in counseling later, I would return to the self-help meetings for families of alcoholics. This time I would be there as a member, not a professional observer, listening and learning how to apply those practical principles in my own life. It was at one of those meetings I heard someone say, "You don't have to go to every argument you are invited to." Although this turned out to be a common expression or slogan at these meetings, I remember my first reaction was, "I never thought of that!"

As a child, I had been taught to stand up for myself and respond if someone made a critical comment or expressed an opinion different from my own. And when I argued, I usually argued to win. Even though I could often help my clients deal with certain concerns in their lives more effectively, I found myself periodically getting caught up in heated arguments with some of the people closest to me. If I reacted in a way I regretted, I tended to be highly critical of myself. After all, I was a professional; I should have been able to practice what I preached. I should have been a better role model. And like a lot of other people who set unrealistic expectations for themselves, I should-ed all over myself. This often resulted in feelings of guilt and remorse. So, being a good over-achiever, I would try "harder" by speaking louder and repeating myself. This typically made me feel more frustrated and less objective, and I usually ended up in the same type of argument anyway.

If You Do What You Always Did, You Will Get What You Always Got

Around the time I started attending those meetings as a member, I was having a conversation with a friend about my father. I was expressing my frustration at my father's inconsistency in following his doctor's orders to watch his diet and take his medicine for high blood pressure. I said something like, "And for the umpteenth time, I told him he needed to do what his doctor said." Calmly and compassionately, she replied, "What did you expect?" I responded with, "For him to offer more excuses just like he always did." Her response caught me off guard: "If he reacted the way you always expected him to, then why did you get into the same conversation?"

There was silence for a few moments while I tried to think. So why *did* I keep having the same conversation? *Well . . . Uh . . .* I hadn't really thought about it before. I was so focused on my father failing to take his medications consistently that I'd lost track of my own actions and reactions. I kept doing the same things over and over with the same results, with both of us getting very upset.

Counselors and therapists dedicate many years to earning two or three college degrees, in addition to fulfilling other requirements for their license. Some become certified or licensed Marital & Family Counselors or Child & Family Counselors. Many will have several areas of focus or specialties, such as dealing with anxiety, depression, substance abuse, trauma, or bereavement. Yet, despite all this training and experience, none of us is immune to the challenges and heartaches that can happen to anyone, nor do professional degrees make life simple or easy.

If you've been struggling in this area, you are not alone. Interactions with others can be very challenging. But as human beings, we can adapt and make changes in the way we communicate. You can continue to develop communication skills that are just as real as the skills an accomplished musician, singer, athlete, or other outwardly successful individual demonstrates. And, in fact, these skills will likely make you a whole lot happier because relationships are the biggest source of happiness. You can also continue to develop additional, tangible coping strategies to help you when you feel like giving up, losing your temper, or avoiding a situation you find overwhelming.

Self-Knowledge Is Power

Years ago, as part of a federal grant, I became trained and certified as a clinical supervisor and counselor in a brief, evidence-based counseling model focused on working with adolescents, called Motivational Enhancement Therapy/Cognitive Behavioral Therapy, 5 sessions, (MET/CBT5).[4]

One of the basic concepts of this approach is understanding that knowledge is power: the more knowledge you have about yourself, the more power you have over your life. I had thought the mantra was from one of the psychologists who had developed and researched that model. A few years later, my wife and I were on vacation in Washington, DC, where we visited the Jefferson Memorial. I noticed a quotation, etched in a marble wall, from Thomas Jefferson, third President of the United States and primary author of the Declaration of Independence: "Knowledge is Power, Knowledge is Happiness."

I agree that self-knowledge is power; the more we learn about ourselves as human beings, the more power it gives us to make better, more informed choices in all aspects of our lives. And being able to more consistently apply what we are learning to our interactions with others significantly increases our potential for true happiness.

It's natural to want to immediately begin with the most pressing and troublesome issues. Many feel a sense of urgency to just "do something" in order to reduce conflicts or heartaches, yet this instinct can actually add to the sense of frustration or hopelessness. Try to take a step back for a moment and think about a time when you learned a new skill—perhaps on the first day of a new job, class, sport, or hobby. Did you begin with one of the most advanced or challenging tasks? Not likely. Even highly qualified professionals need some time to orient to new surroundings, procedures, and routines.

Part of *try different, not harder* is understanding what you would like to be different in your interactions with others. You will learn how to plan and take specific steps along the way to work toward your goals, and to prepare for the human emotions that can sabotage the best of intentions.

Fight, Flight, or Freeze

When faced with high or even moderate levels of stress, the basic neurological response of "fight, flight, or freeze" can kick in. The fight, flight, or freeze response is a combination of survival responses thought to have evolved in humans and other mammals to combat external threats. Your brain signals your two adrenal glands (*ad* meaning "on" and *renal* meaning "kidney," because your adrenals are located on top of your kidneys) to send a hormone, adrenaline, into your bloodstream. Adrenaline in your bloodstream causes your heart to pump blood and oxygen more rapidly throughout your body.

If you are trying to defend yourself from a physical assault, you might find yourself physically stronger than usual (*fight*). If you are running away from a threat, you might find yourself running faster than you thought you could (*flight*). If you perceive a threat and cannot fight or flee, you might lie perfectly still and quiet in the hope of escaping detection (*freeze*). Depending on the circumstances, these responses can be useful; unfortunately, they tend to activate even when they're not needed (like when you're having a heated discussion with someone). When your adrenaline gets flowing in response to everyday life events over and over again, there can be health consequences, as well as damage to your interactions with others.[5]

When you find yourself stuck in fight, flight, or freeze mode, remembering some very simple mnemonic devices can help.

Mnemonics and Other Memory Aids

Mnemonics (pronounced "nemonics") include short phrases, acronyms, initialisms, poems, and even music that can serve as memory aids. They help give meaning to something so you can remember it more easily. You probably used some when you were at school—for example, for the order of the planets: *My Very Educated Mother Just Served Us Noodles (Mercury, Venus, Earth, Mars, Jupiter, Saturn, Uranus, Neptune).*

Examples of one-word mnemonics relevant to our topic are HALT and SOS, which you'll find in Chapter Eight, and FEAR in Chapter Eleven. They remind us of the dangers of becoming overly Hungry, Angry, Lonely, Tired (HALT), or Stressed Out Severely (SOS), and they tell us to Face Everything And Reconcile (FEAR).

Picture yourself in a vehicle traveling down an unfamiliar highway. The road signs—which are usually just one or two words or a symbol—are mnemonic devices designed to direct your attention quickly and safely. If you look at the sign from your side window as you pass it at a high speed, it will probably look like a blur. Is there something wrong with your eyesight? Maybe, but if you slowed down or looked at the sign from another perspective—perhaps through the front windshield—you could probably see the information much more clearly and actually process it. You didn't try harder, you just tried differently, as well as more effectively.

Reminding yourself to "slow down" can help you slow your heart rate, as well as your thinking. This can also help you focus and, with practice, prevent unnecessary "fight, flight, or freeze" responses. You can use these short phrases as self-regulating tools to regulate or moderate anxiety, anger, fear, guilt, and other uncomfortable emotions, preventing them from fueling and escalating disagreements.

Mnemonics and other tools in this book will help you gain valuable perspective into your struggles with others, as well as your emotional reactions. They will help guide you along the road to more productive and rewarding relationships.

Let's begin with the mnemonic of Catching Yourself.

Catch Yourself by Mentally Pressing a Pause Button

Another technique for trying "different, not harder" is learning to "catch yourself."[6] Imagine mentally hitting a pause button before speaking or reacting to what someone else has said or done. This can include a wide range of thoughts and actions, such as the following examples:

- "I bit my lip this time and did not open my mouth when my daughter said that it was so boring to live in our town."

- "I remembered that I had a choice of getting into an argument or not."

With continued insights and practice, you'll start to catch yourself sooner and sooner. As time goes on, you'll also be better able to remember what you want to say and how you want to say it before you speak—even when talking with teenagers! Okay, learning how not to go to every argument your teenager invites you to will probably take more practice—that's why that topic comes later in this book. But try to remember, it takes two to argue!

Many of the values, role models, mnemonic devices, or sayings we were exposed to as children have served us well; after all, we've made it this far. My first recommendation before trying anything different is to identify your strengths—those inner qualities and skills that contribute to your relationship with yourself and with others in healthy ways. Build upon those strengths before trying to make major changes. You might find that you don't need to do something different or try harder; just remember to do what has worked for you in the past.

✎ Take a few moments to record your communication strengths and skills in your journal.

Love is patient, love is kind

Your skills might include being patient, listening well, or having a good sense of humor. Strengths can also include the support you receive from family and friends, or from your faith. Having a hard time listing more than a few things? Write down what you think your friends would say when asked why you're such a good friend. Still having a difficult time? You're not alone. All insurance companies and accreditation organizations (at least all that I am aware of) require counselors to assess, with the client's input, the individual's and (where applicable) other family members' strengths. This allows them to work with each client on an Individualized Action Plan or Counseling Plan.

Clients usually tell me that listing their strengths is one of the most difficult things I ask them to do. Why? Many people feel that talking about their strengths and positive qualities amounts to bragging about themselves, and it can make them feel uncomfortable or even vain. Others are so focused on "what am I doing wrong?" or "what am I missing?" that they simply forget to think about the positive skills, qualities, and strengths they possess. Focusing on your strengths may, for the time being, feel foreign and challenging, but you'll get more comfortable with practice. This simple exercise can make a big difference in how you feel and, ultimately, how you act in the future.

Positive Self-Talk

Find the good in yourself.

Think about an outwardly successful, well-known person whom you admire. Try to picture what this person might be thinking when they are engaged in their work or craft. Can you imagine a successful singer like Lady Gaga walking out on stage and saying to herself *You are not a very good singer*, or a professional baseball player like Mike Trout going up to bat and expecting to strike out each time?

For people who appear before the public, a certain degree of anxiety, at least temporarily, is quite common, even after many years of experience. However, those who have managed to accomplish their goals, despite feeling anxious and pressured, have learned to focus on the tools and skills that have gotten them to where they are today. Who is more likely to accomplish their goal: the Olympic ice skater who focuses on trying to repeat positive body mechanics, or the one who says over and over in their head, *Don't fall down, don't fall down*? Which singer is more likely to have a successful performance: the one who focuses on hitting the note they've rehearsed many times, or the one who stares out on the crowd and gets distracted by thoughts of *Don't mess up, don't mess up*? One common characteristic shared by successful people, in addition to hard work and persistence, is practicing positive self-talk (and also having a strategy for interrupting negative self-talk).

Being outwardly or professionally successful, however, does not automatically mean you possess the knowledge and life skills needed to deal with your own emotions or family, friends, and other personal interactions. Unfortunately, this reality is often played out in the media when a celebrity gets help for an alcohol or drug use disorder, struggles with severe depression and anxiety, or makes very harmful decisions. No amount of money or fame can afford anyone health and happiness.

I have counseled truck drivers, medical professionals, students, an Oscar-winning actor, blue collar workers, white collar workers, and a gold record-winning musician. Regardless of occupation or income, each of us is someone's son or daughter, sister or brother, spouse or partner, colleague or friend, with our own personal strengths and challenges. We all face challenges in life that test us emotionally, and we can all learn from those challenges and improve our skills.

Can you take a few moments to create or expand upon your list of strengths and skills? Here are a few sentence stems to get you started:

- My best friend would say that I am . . .
- I can be . . .

- I like to . . .

- Some of my other strengths and skills are . . .

How did it feel to make a list of your own strengths and skills? Was it very uncomfortable? Somewhat empowering?

- Listing my strengths and skills felt . . .

Before we go on, please complete the following sentence stems. Notice that they are directed at what you have learned about yourself and what you want to do.

- I learned that I . . .

- I would like to . . .

- I can begin to do that by . . .

- Things I want to remember or focus on are . . .

Pick Your Priorities

Do you really want to spend a great deal of your time and energy arguing about things like who left the cap off the toothpaste tube, who forgot to turn the light off when they left the room, or how no one seems to know the correct way to load a dishwasher except you?

When you are visiting someone who is sick or injured in a hospital, or when you're celebrating the birth of a baby, how important is the dirty dish left in the sink, the misplaced television remote, or some other common annoying occurrence? When you find yourself tempted to complain about something that annoys you, it can be helpful to ask yourself, "How important is it?"

Remember, since undesirable patterns are formed through repetition, you will need to repeat mnemonic devices such as *How important is it?* to retrain your thinking patterns. How many times and how often will you need to repeat these memory aids? I have no idea. I do know that none of us developed our strengths and skills overnight—we had to earn them! With practice and follow-through, you can continue to build upon those strengths and skills. A mnemonic that might help is, "I'll keep trying one step at a time."

Moving Forward

Take a moment to jot down your priorities in life. What's most important and meaningful to you? Now think back to a recent situation that annoyed or frustrated you. How important is that situation compared to what's most important to you?

Scooby Doo!
Wow!. Far out!
Don't get hooked!

I would like to look back on this as an opportunity for growth, peace + togetherness

CHAPTER FOUR

You Don't Have to Invite Yourself (or Others) to Arguments

In a relationship where there is an emotional bond or other ongoing interaction, including at work and certainly among politicians, I suggest no one ever really wins a heated argument. The hurt that is felt in a heated argument can last a long time, long after passions have cooled, or the issue no longer remains. That's why in most cases, it's better to concentrate on working together to resolve a disagreement rather than to fight.

Working Instead of Fighting

Many of us have learned to fight for what we believe in, to not give up, and to persevere when we're faced with obstacles. But this persistence—this habit of fighting and never giving up—can lead to arguments, because our behavior might make others think we're too stubborn or aggressive. Aggressive comments tend to trigger either defensive or aggressive reactions from others.

Some of us have learned to avoid conflict, giving us a short-term respite from arguments, but eventually we may find our emotions building up and periodically boiling over when we can't handle it anymore. These emotions might leak out in a sarcastic tone of voice or through slammed doors.

Whether you tend to face conflict and challenges head-on or avoid them, you can learn to build upon your current strengths and modify the way you approach disagreements instead of viewing every situation as all-or-nothing. You can work for what you believe in instead of fighting for it.

When you decide to work instead of fight, it changes everything! Like tossing a pebble into a pond, every positive action you take to change your communication with others also has a ripple effect. This creates a dynamic of positive interactions and self-reinforcing behaviors that will make your relationships more pleasant and less stressful over time.

Don't give up. Persevere and continue to build more effective communication skills and disagreement-management techniques. If you typically avoid conflict, you'll learn to identify the concerns that may have led you to avoid certain conversations, and if you tend to be persistent, you'll discover new ways to express yourself so that emotions do not have to build to volatile levels.

Be Proactive Instead of Reactive

I will be tested today . . .

When you focus on what another person has said or done (or not done), and how they have spoken or acted, you give control of your emotions to someone else. When you react to criticism or perceived criticism, you put yourself on the defensive. The reality is that you're human and you can only control 50 percent of any discussion: what you say, and the manner in which you respond.[7] You do not have to like what the other person has said or how they said it, but when you focus on what you want to say and how you can communicate it so that it will be heard by others, you gain control of yourself, your emotions, your thoughts, and your actions. You'll also gain self-respect.

By shifting your focus, you can alter your results. When you anticipate difficult issues and plan specific actions for a more desirable outcome, you are being proactive. Conversely, when something happens that you had not anticipated or were not adequately prepared for, you will likely be reactive. If you find yourself being reactive, call a time-out and give yourself a little bit of time to prepare for the conversation so you can handle it to the best of your abilities, using all your strengths and skills, combined with some journaling, insights, and forethought.

Most of us find a proactive approach less stressful and therefore more desirable in the long run, but it's not always possible to foresee every situation that could provoke an argument. So, try to take a few deep breaths as you continue to develop strategies for anticipating specific argument "triggers" and high-risk situations. As we continue, you'll learn even more strategies for catching yourself when you didn't anticipate a high-risk situation, or when you're just being human and are overwhelmed by your emotions.

When You're Tired of Fighting

People waste inordinate amounts of time and energy trying hard to force a resolution when there's a difference of opinion. When you repeat the same actions over and over and get the same unsatisfactory results, you can develop a type of tunnel vision where you have difficulty seeing or considering alternatives.[8] Being tired can make you more stressed and more likely to argue, just as arguing more can cause you to become stressed and tired. This feedback loop can sometimes get out of hand, and it can be very hard on your physical and mental health, as well as your relationships. I cannot tell you how to get more energy to deal with all your relationship concerns or how to get more hours in a day. However, together we can strategize on how to redirect your time and energy more effectively.

My first recommendation if you suffer from persistent fatigue, insomnia, poor appetite, or other physical concerns is to make an appointment with your primary care physician.

Your doctor can determine if there is a physical explanation or if you are experiencing depression, anxiety, or some other condition. They will either provide specific treatment or refer you to another professional for additional assessment and help. Regardless of whether you get a diagnosis or what the diagnosis is, you'll likely find, as many others have, that arguing less makes you feel like you have more energy to do the things in life you really want to do.

In the past I have found, usually after much frustration and aggravation, that I wasted a great deal of energy trying to change the things I couldn't in dealing with family or other *yup* interpersonal interactions. At times, I focused on what other people said and did—or did not say and do. I often dwelt on the "if onlys": "If only I had remembered to say this instead of that." Or the "what ifs": "What if I say this and she says that . . ." and it went on and on. Initially, some suggestions I heard at my self-help meetings seemed more overwhelming than helpful. It seemed that for every step forward, I would take several steps back.

Along the way, someone told me I didn't have to like the fact that I couldn't change many of the things I thought were so vitally important; but if I directed my energy and focus to *Stoic* what I *could* change, the change would indeed happen. Once I slowly began to accept this, I started to feel better and more hopeful. I decided to start with changing me—my behavior, thoughts, and habitual responses. Once I recognized it was in my own best interest to keep learning whatever I could to grow as a person, things, in fact, began to change. As I changed how I spoke to others, I began to feel less angry, more calm, and able to think more clearly. I also began to notice that certain people were responding positively to the way I was now speaking to them.

I think we would all agree that we can't change the past or the weather, but how often do we worry about whether it will rain on our day off or some other day that is important to us? Intellectually, it would seem very easy to accept that we cannot change the past or the weather, but emotional acceptance is quite another matter. How much time and energy have we wasted dwelling on what someone has said or done?

It has been said that nature abhors a vacuum. Think about the sound you hear when you open a new jar of pickles: that "pop" is the sudden rush of air filling the vacuum that's left in the canning process. When you're trying to change an undesirable behavior or trait, focus on replacing it with a more desirable one. As you redirect your focus to what you *can* change, the old, less desirable behaviors no longer rush to fill the void; instead, your new behaviors are reinforced.

Focusing on what you can change or influence also develops hope and encouragement for continued efforts and progress. But just because you can't force change in others doesn't mean you have to accept unacceptable behavior; this will be discussed further in Chapter Seven, *You Don't Have to Keep Arguing with Yourself.*

When You Feel Stuck

How familiar are you with comments like these?

- "He doesn't care."
- "She did it on purpose."
- "Why should I try? They won't ever change."

I have heard comments like these from many people over the years. What each person usually has in common at this point—whether they be a husband, wife, boyfriend, girlfriend, parent, adult child, close friend, or coworker—is significant frustration and emotional pain. The pain may result from repeated, unsuccessful efforts to improve their relationships.

It may come from periods of feeling discouraged, or just feeling stuck. During many of my counseling sessions with couples and families, when everyone appeared stuck and initially unable to identify any areas of agreement, I've offered this observation:

> "I can see, literally, each of you in front of me. That communicates to me an agreement that the status quo is not acceptable and, perhaps to some degree, some hope that maybe, just maybe, something might help bring about some positive change."

This may also apply to you when you feel deeply concerned about your relationship with a parent, sibling, or once-close friend. You might feel like they just don't care enough to change, listen, or have that conversation you want to have. But if they show up to an argument, that means they do care enough. So instead of focusing on them and what they're doing wrong, you can redirect your focus to the things you can change to improve your interaction with them.

Picture a beautiful spring day. It's your day off, and you have just awakened after having the best night's sleep. The sun is shining, the birds are singing, and you feel great! Your spouse walks in from another room with a big smile on their face and says, "Good morning! How do you feel this morning?" Just as they're speaking, you accidentally bang your big toe hard against the table leg.

Is the sun still shining? Are the birds still singing? Did you not have a wonderful night's sleep? It doesn't seem to matter at that moment, because the only thing you are aware of is the half-inch on the end of your toe that that hurts so badly you can't think straight. Pain is nature's way of getting your attention so that you take care of yourself and take action to prevent further physical or emotional harm. Until you tend to the immediate issue (in this case, your big toe) and the pain subsides, you may be unable to accurately assess other physical or emotional feelings.

Relationship discord can and often does result in degrees of emotional pain, especially if you're stuck on what the other person is doing or not doing. Once you return your focus back to what you can change—including how you respond to others and how you take care of *your* needs—your relationships will often improve noticeably because you will feel less emotional pain when you change the focus from things you can't control to things you can. And just as you'll be better able to respond when your toe doesn't hurt so much, you'll also be better able to respond when your emotions don't hurt so much.

Another Freakin' Growth Experience

Throughout my career, four of my supervisors were psychologists, or doctoral-level non-physician therapists. I have learned a great deal from them. During my weekly one-hour supervision session with one of them, Doctor John P. McPeake, I presented for discussion what I thought was a very challenging case. It involved a client who was only slowly making progress, and I was exhausted from racking my brain for insights into his problems. Doctor McPeake's response to me was a cryptic "AFGE." Thinking it was an abbreviation for some psychological diagnosis I was not familiar with, I asked him what it meant. He replied, "Another freakin' growth experience," which caught me quite by surprise. He went on to say that sometimes you can learn a great deal from a very challenging or painful situation. Tough times can also motivate you to deal more effectively with similar issues in the future, and to be more vigilant in preventing similar experiences.

If only we human beings could learn all of life's lessons quickly and without stress or strain. Personally, I am tired of learning things the hard way, yet every so often, I still manage to cut myself while slicing a roll, or do or say something I regret and immediately think afterward, "Darn it, Jerry, not again!" But I am getting better, and I intend to keep learning. Reportedly, Albert Einstein's favorite quotation, which he had on the wall of his office at Princeton University, was Mahatma Gandhi's "Live as if you would die tomorrow. Learn as if you will live forever."

Challenge yourself to keep learning so you can catch yourself sooner and prevent more heated arguments. When you're going through something really difficult and painful, remember that it's just another freakin' growth experience, that you still have more to learn, and that you *will* learn if you focus on what you can change.

Don't Send Mixed Messages

"I can't hear what you are saying when you talk so loud."

Communication involves more than words alone. Whether you are consciously aware of it or not, you communicate in a variety of ways. How many times have you found yourself reacting to someone's tone of voice, the volume of their speech, or the signals from their body language? Their words convey one message, but their decibel level, facial expression, or pointed finger sends a very different one. Remembering that you're both human can help you listen beyond the tone of their voice and see past their animated body language. What if they were annoyed over something that happened at work, worried about a loved one's recent medical crisis, or even feeling ill themselves, and their tone actually had nothing to do with you or the immediate conversation?

Hand and head gestures can have a variety of meanings,

depending on your culture. There are also generational and regional variations within cultures, and countless other non-verbal cues that have different meanings. Daniel R. Stalder, a social psychologist and professor of psychology at the University of Wisconsin-Whitewater, states that while some people can more accurately "decode" or interpret non-verbal body language, "Most of us think we're better than average, when really only about half of us can be."[9] In other words, we're overly confident in our ability to decode nonverbal communication. It's all too easy to think we can read someone when we can't, and we're often too quick to take offense and criticize.

Men's and Women's Brains Are Wired Differently

One beautiful summer's day, I headed out with my good friend and kayaking partner, John M., to the quaint town of Hancock in southwestern New Hampshire. Shortly before reaching our destination, we realized I had forgotten to bring the directions to the lake, and John had left his GPS at home. As we pulled into the center of town, which consisted of numerous white clapboard colonial homes, two wooden churches, and one small grocery store, I volunteered to go into the store and ask for directions (yes, men *are* able to ask for directions).

I walked up to the counter and asked the woman standing there, "Can you tell me how to get to Spoonwood Lake?" She and a female customer, in a very friendly way, directed me to turn left when I exited the store. As they were describing several landmarks I would encounter along the way, a male customer entered. Overhearing part of our conversation and recognizing the glazed, confused look on my face, he asked me, "Where are you heading to?" I explained that my friend and I planned to go kayaking on Spoonwood Lake. He pointed to a map of the town under a sheet of glass on the countertop under my left hand. He said, "We are here. Turn left when you leave the store, which is heading west. Drive for about one and a half miles, and then turn left on [such and such] road. Take your first right and continue until you come to the boat landing." My glazed, confused look disappeared, and John and I were on our way to a great afternoon's paddle.

Now, if a female kayaker had gone into the same store and asked the male customer for directions to Spoonwood Lake, she might just as well have developed a confused, bewildered look of her own at the man's directions. The female clerk might have recognized that look and described, in great detail, the various landmarks on the way to the lake, and the kayaker most likely would have been happily on her way. What the heck is going on here?

Research by Ragini Verma and others from the Perelman School of Medicine suggests that men's and women's brains are wired differently, which means they do not always think the same way.[10] (But you probably didn't need a scientist to tell you that, did you?) This may help explain differences in communication styles between the sexes. For example, women, on average, often appear better than men at remembering words and faces, as well as creating solutions that work for a group. Men, on average, appear to be better at learning and performing a single task at hand, such as navigation and sensorimotor speed.

With modern, non-invasive tools such as MRI (Magnetic Resonance Imaging) and DTI (Diffusion Tensor Imaging), scientists are learning more about the human brain at a faster rate than ever before. This gives us more insight into how we function and behave from physiological, psychological, and communication perspectives. But while technology helps us in many ways to lead more productive and informed lives, it will never solve all the mysteries of life, such as fully understanding the opposite sex or accomplishing world peace. What we do know is that the average man and the average woman process information, experience the world, and communicate differently. We also know that each person is unique, so assuming that anyone you're talking to (or married to) processes information, experiences the world, or communicates the same way you do is likely to lead you astray. Assuming you know someone else's thoughts or motives will send you into an emotional relationship minefield.

Instead of assuming what someone else is thinking, which will only frustrate you more, try something different: ask them. Likewise, if you want someone to know how you are feeling, communicate your emotions and concerns with positive and concise words, rather than slamming doors, giving someone the silent treatment, or expecting your loved ones to know intuitively how you feel. Don't assume you know what someone else is thinking or that they know what you're thinking, because their brain is probably very different from yours.

Working Together to Create Change

Most of us would probably agree that teachers do not make students learn—they cooperate with parents to motivate, stimulate, and guide students in learning and growing. In theory, that's all well and good. However, when it's your son or daughter who is struggling with a subject, your own efforts to support and encourage them can easily cross over into trying too hard to help. Even when you approach a situation with good intentions, someone else might perceive your efforts as interfering or coming on too strongly. This may be the single most important aspect of not inviting yourself or someone else to arguments, whether it be a spouse, partner, parent, sibling, child, close friend, or even a coworker. Are you trying to influence or help someone to understand your feelings and point of view, or are you trying to make someone understand you? The following could be indications that you're trying to make someone understand you or change their point of view.

Do you find yourself:

- Repeating yourself more than once?
- Raising your voice as if the other person doesn't hear you?
- Telling someone what they should or shouldn't do?

Here are some additional points to think about:

- Consider that there may be two sides to an issue.
- Consider that there may be more than two sides to an issue.
- Consider that one person isn't necessarily right and the other wrong.
- Consider eliminating the words "right" and "wrong" when discussing opinions, and instead acknowledge that each person has their own "perspective" or "view."
- Consider that others are entitled to their own opinions. You don't have to agree with them, nor do you have to disagree.
- Consider that you do not need to have an opinion on every issue or subject right now, or ever. You can simply say, "I don't know," or "I need to think about that and get back to you."

Conflicts in the Workplace—Working It Out

Do you get tired of fixing your coworkers' mistakes? How much time do you spend rehashing points of disagreements in meetings? According to The Global Human Capital Report, in an extensive research project, five thousand full-time employees in Europe and the Americas were asked about conflicts in their workplaces. In their responses, 85 percent said they had to deal with conflicts to some degree, and 29 percent said they always or frequently did.[11]

Constructively dealing with conflicts and disagreements can lead to a better understanding of others, which in turn can lead to major innovations and solutions. Considering that you probably spend more time with your coworkers than you do with your family and friends, improving your communication and coping skills with certain coworkers can significantly improve your productivity and the quality of your life. Some conflicts may just be the result of annoying habits, including perhaps your own. We will address strategies for identifying and changing your own habits in Chapters Seven and Eight.

Ask For Help

Instead of venting your frustrations about a coworker to your supervisor or manager, ask for your supervisor or manager's input. Describing it as a customer service issue, production process, or other problem, instead of complaining about a person's attitude or behavior, is more likely to elicit a supportive response.

At times, your manager may suggest taking your concern to the Human Resources Department. You may also choose to approach HR if talking with your manager and your coworker does not satisfactorily resolve the matter. Speaking with someone in HR may also be appropriate if you cannot

resolve ongoing disagreements that directly inv(
supervisor. Again, you're more likely to get supp
you are specific and present your concerns in a co
manner, rather than venting. In the study mentioned above,
63 percent of workers said they were satisfied with how their
HR department dealt with conflict resolution.

Defuse Conflicts on Social Media

In today's digital age, you can be invited to arguments
on a variety of platforms and devices, sometimes by people
you don't even know. With the tap of a finger, social media
can become an instant battleground, but it also offers an
opportunity to use your communication and emotional-
coping skills to connect with many people.

Instead of reacting to a provocative comment on social
media, you can plan strategies to defuse the matter. For
example, you could use a time-out to help calm your emotions.
You might then post a positive and respectful comment,
giving your point of view clearly but without arguing. Or, you
could message the person directly, text them, or, even better,
talk with them. Sometimes talking directly with the person is
more likely to ensure your concern is heard. You can remind
yourself that trying to score points increases defensiveness in
others, while choosing to work instead of fight for what you
believe in does more to promote meaningful change.

Focusing on what you can control—your thoughts,
feelings, and actions—can help you use the tools of social
media to set healthier boundaries when you find certain
posts offensive or otherwise inappropriate. Most social media
platforms give you options to manage what types of posts
you prefer not to see. For example, you can activate certain
settings to see fewer posts that you find unacceptable, and
you can choose to hide posts even when you agree with the

opinion but find the presentation offensive, shaming, vulgar, or otherwise counter-productive. You can also choose to hide or block all posts from specific individuals or groups. Lastly, you can block all contact with certain people.

Scoring Points

Leave point-scoring to athletic contests and other competitive games. Focusing on all the reasons why your opinion is right or the other person's is wrong is like playing with matches near a pile of crumpled-up newspapers and dried leaves; it's usually just a matter of time before one of the matches starts a heated blaze.

Depending on your relationship to the other person or the subject matter, a focus on scoring points usually results in an increasingly heated exchange, with each person defending their position and trying to prove that the other is mistaken, invalid, completely ignorant, and . . . *oh boy, there I go again.* When you focus on scoring points, you also keep the argument going inside your head.

When Your Ex Is Also the Parent of Your Child

You can break up with a partner or divorce a spouse, but if you have a child or children together, you'll probably need to maintain some communication with your ex. Unfortunately, many break-ups do not end amicably, but you can adapt the techniques in this book to fit your specific situation.

Text Your Ex

Many of my separated or divorced clients have found it helpful to text or e-mail their ex in lieu of face-to-face or telephone contact. This helps in several ways. First, it gives each parent the opportunity to communicate messages or questions, usually about their children, without having to hear the other parent's voice, either live or in a recorded message. It also gives each parent time to process the information (and yell into a pillow, cry if needed, tear up old photos, contact a friend or relative for support, or vent however they want to) without having to immediately react. Later, they can text or e-mail their response in a more calm, straightforward, and constructive manner.

Written communication can minimize the need to rely on your selective memory, and can serve as a helpful, matter-of-fact reminder of appointments or school functions and, if needed, document compliance or noncompliance with court-mandated child support, visitation, and other legal matters. You also can use the time between written communications to review what you have written and use some of the tools you are learning in the best interests of your children, as well as yourself. Texting or e-mailing can be a viable, proactive way of communicating with anyone when you need time to think, calm your emotions, and not invite yourself or others to an argument.

This Is the Time

This is the time for each of us to communicate more effectively and find some common ground. You can increase the likelihood of your concerns really being heard not by raising the volume of your voice, but by raising the level of your communication and listening skills, while also better managing your emotions. You can begin practicing this one conversation at a time, with your spouse or partner, your parent or child, another family member, a friend, a coworker, and the next person you interact with. *This* is the time.

✎ Moving Forward

Answer the following questions in your journal:

- When you focus your thoughts on what you don't like about someone's behaviors, or how they are not doing what you think they should be doing, how do you feel?

- When you focus your thoughts on what you *can* change, how do you feel?

- Here's what I can do to improve my relationship with [insert name]:

CHAPTER FIVE

Get Your Concerns Really Heard

As you continue to improve your communication and emotional coping skills, you'll send fewer mixed messages and get your concerns really heard.

In 2009, as part of a federal grant, I participated in a three-day training led by Robert J. Meyers, along with eight other counselors. Afterward, I started adapting some of his work with families of substance abusers to help my own clients more effectively deal with the common, everyday challenges in their relationships. Dr. Meyers, a former research professor of psychology at the University of New Mexico, helped develop the Community Reinforcement And Family Training (CRAFT) model. The CRAFT model uses scientifically validated principles, including Positive Communication, to teach family members and other Concerned Significant Others (CSOs) the communication skills they need to influence improvement in their relationship with the drinker or substance user in their lives. It assists family members and CSOs with influencing—not controlling—the reduction of the loved one's substance use, and encouraging the person, in most cases, to seek treatment. It also helps family members and CSOs reduce their own anxiety, depression, anger, and physical concerns.[12]

Seven Guidelines for Positive Communication

The overriding principle of Positive Communication (and this book) is that positive, respectful, non-confrontational communication is more likely to get you the result you want: to have your concerns really heard and considered. How you speak to others—your tone of voice, as well as your choice of words—can also make it easier for others to "save face" when they are reevaluating their own opinions or actions, while making them less defensive and more open to your point of view.

Positive Communication is mutually empowering, and also contagious.[13] It has seven guidelines: be brief; be positive and non-confrontational; refer to a specific behavior; label your emotions; offer an understanding statement; accept partial responsibility; and offer to help.

You don't have to use all seven of these helpful tools in every conversation. If you find certain aspects of Positive Communication more difficult to use or initially buy into, you can start with what does work for you and build from there. It can be helpful to practice using positive and respectful communication with a specific friend or sibling, especially if you tend to have difficulty expressing yourself in an assertive, non-aggressive way. Your friend or sibling may enjoy playing the role of your spouse, partner, parent, child, teen, boss, or coworker. Counselors often use role-play to help clients gain insights into issues, as well as to practice skills before using them in real-life situations. Have your journal handy to record thoughts, insights, and questions as they come to mind during the role-play. Think of this as a rehearsal before the big show, or practice before the big game. Try to remember: successful people repeatedly work on the skills that bring successful outcomes. *Practice makes progress.*

For each of the sections that follow, return to your answers from the *Why do I argue? Self-Questionnaire* in Chapter One. Look at your answers to identify changes you'd like to make in your interactions. You can also add other past comments that you'd like to replace with better ways of getting your concerns heard, and practice recording new comments that demonstrate your progress for each of the seven guidelines of Positive

Communication. Allow for extra space to change, adapt, and add to your responses as additional concerns or ideas come up.

Many people find it helpful to have some notes written down before starting a discussion with another person. Use a few keywords or short sentences, and leave extra space between phrases and lines to help your eyes focus. It's certainly okay to write out each word you wish to say and read them directly. A brief proactive statement, such as "Our relationship is very important to me, so I wrote down a few notes to help me better communicate my thoughts and feelings," clarifies this new approach. When you're just starting out, try using your new communication skills with smaller, less stressful concerns, rather than starting with the most emotionally-charged ones. This can be part of *trying different, not harder.*

Remember: there are no magic words to use. As you develop your communication skills and continue to gain more insights, you will become less anxious and more comfortable in your exchanges with others.

Now let's look at the seven guidelines of Positive Communication in more detail:

Be Brief

Think KISS—Keep It Simple, Sweetheart (another mnemonic). More is not always better, especially when emotions may be running high or have the potential to escalate. Once you get into a long explanation, you'll often end up repeating your point or introducing additional concerns and examples. This increases the likelihood of the other person becoming defensive or distracted. Instead, being brief puts you in a better position to focus on what you want to say, as well as how you want to say it. Try to remember to discuss just one concern at a time.

Let's look at some examples.

Examples of Being Brief

Prior long-version attempt: "The dishes are piling up in the sink again. They're beginning to turn colors and they stink. I hope no one comes to visit us and sees this mess! The last time that happened, I was mortified. I don't know why I have to keep reminding you about this."

Progress in being brief: "You didn't have a chance to do the dishes before? Can you get started on them in the next few minutes? Thanks."

Prior long-version attempt: "We don't go out anywhere together anymore. All I seem to do is get up and go to work. I come home and it's one problem after another. All I do is work, work, work. I can't stand it anymore!"

Progress in being brief: "I miss spending time with you alone. Let's get a babysitter and go out to see a movie Saturday."

Prior long-version attempt: "I am sick and tired of having to pick up after you all the time. I am not your maid! How much effort does it take to put your dirty clothes where they belong? And another thing, you said you'd take care of *yada, yada, yada*, and you would also do 'such and such' by Tuesday, and it is already Thursday. And I . . ."

Progress in being brief: "You forgot to put the soiled clothes in the hamper. Can you please do that now, so it's done?"

✎ Your Turn

(If more examples come to mind, feel free to write more than one.)

- My prior long-version comment:
- My progress in being brief comment:

Be Positive

Use positive statements to communicate what you would like to see happen instead of telling others what you don't like. When you do this, it gives others a better understanding of what you expect of them. Just imagine how you would respond if someone approached you in a positive, respectful, and non-confrontational manner, as opposed to an aggressive, accusatory one. Using positive, non-confrontational, and respectful words can also reduce the other person's defensiveness, and potentially your own, on the off chance that you are mistaken *(but of course that couldn't be!)*.

Examples of Being Positive

Prior confrontational attempt: "I can't stand it when you show up forty-five minutes late and make me worried sick."

Progress being positive, non-confrontational, and respectful: "I get really worried when you are very late, and I don't know where you are. I would appreciate it if you would call or text me to let me know if you are going to be late. Thanks."

Prior confrontational attempt: "Don't tell me what I should or shouldn't do!"

Progress in being positive, non-confrontational, and respectful: "I appreciate your feedback, as I value your opinions. I find I am more open to comments when they are presented in the form of ideas or suggestions."

Prior confrontational attempt [to a customer service representative]: "This product of yours is a piece of junk!!"

Progress in being positive, non-confrontational, and respectful: Have your questions written down, as well as the make and model number of the product before making the phone call. Remind yourself that the customer service person is not the reason for your problem. When the person introduces themselves, write down their name—e.g., "Mike"—and say,

"Hi, Mike, my name is Ed and I need your help with my . . ."

Prior confrontational comment: "It's so rude to be on your cellphone while we are talking."

Progress in being positive, non-confrontational, and respectful: "If you need to finish what you are doing on your phone, can we take a break and arrange a time to talk later?"

Prior confrontational comment: "OK, but make sure you bring it back this time!"

Progress in being positive, non-confrontational, and respectful: "OK, but I will need to use it again soon. I'd really appreciate it if you would make a note to return this to me by four o'clock. Thanks."

Prior confrontational attempt: "Your music is too loud. I'm trying to work here!"

Progress in being positive, non-confrontational, and respectful [said in private if you're at work]: "Bob, please use your earbuds or close your office door when you are listening to music. I'd really appreciate it. Thanks."

✐ Your Turn

Again, feel free to write more than one set of examples in your journal:

- My prior confrontational comment:

- My positive, non-confrontational, and respectful comment:

Be Specific

Referring to a specific concern, rather than making a broad statement, is likely to result in more effective discussions and responses. Asking someone to change a certain behavior is a more identifiable concern and can be positively reinforced.

Try to catch yourself before you use generalizations such as *always, never, everyone,* and *no one.* When you assume you know what someone else is thinking or feeling and say things like, "You think you're so much smarter than everyone else," or "You feel so picked on whenever I try to discuss something," you're inviting yourself and the other person to jump right into an argument.

Examples of Being Specific

Prior broad statement attempt: "Why am I the one who always has to keep track of everything around here?"

Progress referring to a specific concern: "I would like your help deciding which bills to pay first. Can we pick a time to go over them?"

Prior broad statement attempt: "Things have got to change around here and change fast!"

Progress referring to a specific concern: "I need to call a time-out to simmer down before I lose it big time!" You go for a walk, practice other types of self-care (as we'll discuss in Chapter Eight), review "Letting go of anger and resentments" in Chapter Seven, and review any other sections of this book as needed. Sometime later you say: "I would like to pick a time to talk about [insert specific topic]…"

Your Turn

- My prior broad statement:

- My attempt referring to a specific concern comment:

Label Your Emotions

Other people are more likely to acknowledge your emotions open-mindedly and empathize with you when you present your concerns calmly and without blame. Expecting loved ones to know how you feel will create a vicious cycle of maddening conversations inside your own head, as well as relentless arguments with yourself and others.

Be careful to make sure you're actually sharing your feelings and not just your opinions when you label your emotions. A comment such as "I feel that this is unfair" offers your opinion but doesn't communicate much about your emotions. Your opinion is your opinion—it may be valid, but it is different from a feeling. While "good" and "bad" are feeling words, they don't communicate how someone is feeling as effectively as many of the feeling words listed below. Using feeling words to label your emotions will help you to communicate more accurately and clearly.

The following is a partial list of feeling words that can help you to label your emotions so you can communicate them to others and encourage mutual connection, understanding, and empathy.

- *Uncomfortable emotions:* afraid, aggravated, angry, annoyed, anxious, blamed, bothered, confused, depressed, disappointed, distressed, embarrassed, frustrated, guilty, irritated, lonely, nervous, overwhelmed, regretful, sad, tired, uncomfortable.

- *Pleasant, agreeable emotions:* amazed, at ease, calm, comfortable, confident, excited, fortunate, glad, happy, hopeful, inspired, joyful, loved, loving, motivated, peaceful, pleased, proud, relaxed, sensitive, thankful, warm, wonderful, satisfied.

- *Neutral emotions:* affected, concerned, surprised, unsure.

Examples of Labeling Emotions

Prior attempt without labeling your emotions: "I feel that this is unfair."

Progress in labeling your emotions calmly, without judgment or blame: "I feel angry and frustrated because this seems unfair to me."

Prior attempt without labeling your emotions: "Why do you do things like that?!"

Progress in labeling your emotions calmly, without judgment or blame: "When you criticize me in front of others, I feel hurt and embarrassed."

Prior attempt without labeling your emotions: "Sometimes you act as if you are the only one who lives here!"

Progress in labeling your emotions calmly, without judgment or blame: "Please remember to put the seat down after you use the toilet. I feel angry when you leave the seat up. I went to sit down and got a very cold surprise."

Prior attempt without labeling your emotions: "Don't interrupt me!"

Progress in labeling your emotions calmly, without judgment or blame: Speak to the other person later, at a calmer time, in private. "I feel annoyed when you interrupt me while I am talking on the phone. Please touch my free hand or signal me to get my attention and I will ask you what you need as soon as I can."

Your Turn

- My prior comment not labeling my emotions:
- How I could communicate my emotions briefly, calmly, without judgment or blame:

Offer an Understanding Statement

Showing that you understand, or are trying to understand, what another person is saying or feeling can help them feel less need to defend their position. As you start to catch yourself before reacting to differences of opinion or certain comments, show others that you are trying to understand what they're saying or feeling. It's one of the most powerful ways to connect with another human being.

I usually try to avoid saying "I know how you feel" to other people, especially to a teenager. Such a response has the potential to trivialize the other person's experience, and you might not fully understand what they're actually going through. Instead, you could say something like, "Can you help me understand what you are feeling?" or, "When you are ready to tell me, I really would like to know what you are feeling." This demonstrates your willingness to understand and help improve the situation, but without making the conversation about your own experiences.

Examples of Offering an Understanding Statement

Prior attempt: "You shouldn't feel embarrassed by what other people say about you. They are not really your friends anyway."

Progress in offering an understanding statement: "Sometimes people can seem pretty cruel and insensitive. I'm glad you feel you can talk with me about it."

Prior comment: "When I want your advice, I'll ask for it!"

Progress in offering an understanding statement: "I understand that you want what's best for me and are only trying to help. I am usually more open to others asking if I would like some help, rather than receiving unsolicited advice."

Prior comment: "You are making too much noise!"

Progress in offering an understanding statement: "I appreciate the need to have fun with friends. Can you use your indoor voices?" Or, "Can we reach some compromise on the volume of the music?"

Prior attempt: "No intelligent person would say things like that!" or, "How can you believe that?"

Progress offering an understanding statement and being positive, non-confrontational, and respectful: "It seems both of us feel very strongly about this. I value you as a [friend, brother, coworker, etc.]. Can we agree to disagree and talk about something else for now?"

Prior attempt: "You're late for our joint project. Now I'm going to have to rush to complete my part."

Progress in offering an understanding statement: "I know things can get pretty intense around here. Help me understand how you got behind schedule so I might be able to help if this happens again." If they respond with a standard, "It won't happen again," you can follow up with, "I'm not here to judge. But, since we work together, we can also help each other when things start getting hectic."

Your Turn

- My prior comment:

- My progress in offering an understanding statement:

Accept Partial Responsibility

Accepting partial responsibility when appropriate, even a small part, can often take the wind out of an argument before it gets rolling. This shows that you don't consider yourself perfect, and that you're not trying to scapegoat the other person. It also communicates that you're willing to examine your role in the matter, as well as work together to resolve or reduce conflicts.

Examples of Taking Partial Responsibility

Prior comment not accepting partial responsibility: "Why didn't you check to see if Johnny had finished his homework last night while I was working late?"

Progress in accepting partial responsibility: "I know I contribute to our arguments, especially when it's about the children. I love you and I am trying to learn how to express my thoughts and feelings in more effective ways. Can you tell me what happened with Johnny and his homework last night?"

Prior comment not accepting partial responsibility: "You spend money like it grows on trees."

Progress in accepting partial responsibility: "I am concerned about our finances. I know I don't always realize how much I spend between paychecks. Can we pick a day and time to try to get a better idea of where our money is spent?"

Prior comment not accepting partial responsibility: "I can't stand it when you are on your cellphone while we are talking."

Progress in accepting partial responsibility: "I know I can get carried away at times with what I want to say, and I hope you didn't feel left out of the conversation. If you need to check your phone, I hope you will join in as soon as you are done."

Prior comment not accepting partial responsibility: "I am tired of you always saying you're too tired to make love."

Progress in accepting partial responsibility: "I am sorry that I have been so [preoccupied, insensitive, etc.], and I realize I need to contribute more to rekindling our love life, including helping out more around here. Where can I start?"

Prior attempt at not accepting partial responsibility: "You don't even know what you are talking about! And another thing . . ."

Progress in accepting partial responsibility: "I know I can get carried away when we talk about politics. Can we make this a politics-free workplace, so none of us wind up with a stroke or bad case of indigestion?"

✎ Your Turn

- My prior comment where I didn't take partial responsibility:

- How I could communicate my partial responsibility:

Offer to Help

Offering to help in a calm, straightforward way is more likely to get the results you want than if you're just critical. While the other person may be open to a specific type of assistance, offering help in a more general way will likely be seen as supportive and non-critical.

Examples of Offering to Help

Prior attempt: "Let me do that for you."

Progress in offering to help: "Can I be of some help in any way?"

Prior attempt: You start to clean, fix, or move objects without asking if the other person needs help or where things belong.

Progress in offering to help: "How might I be of some help?"

- My prior comment offering to help:
- My progress in offering to help:

How You Begin Your Statements Matters

Beginning your statements with "I" and making direct eye contact helps to assert your thoughts and opinions clearly, respectfully, directly, and without confrontation. In contrast, statements that begin with "you" can be interpreted as aggressive and confrontational, and are more likely to be received with defensiveness, retaliation, or avoidance.

Beginning with "Well, I," while avoiding eye contact is an example of unassertive or passive communication, and signals to others that you aren't really confident in what you're saying.

"Aggressive You" and "Assertive I" Examples

Prior "aggressive you" comment: "You should call me if you are going to be late coming home instead of just showing up and making me worried sick."

Progress in being assertive: "I get really worried when you are late coming home and I do not know where you are. I would appreciate it if you would call or text me to let me know if you are going to be more than a few minutes late."

Prior "aggressive you" comment: "You have no right to yell at me like that!"

Progress in being assertive: "I would be happy to talk with you when you are able to discuss this issue without yelling." Then, if the other person is unable to talk more calmly, call a time-out and walk away in a respectful manner.

Prior "aggressive you" comment: "You need to be more considerate of other people's workspace." (The word "need" is usually interpreted as a command and causes a defensive reaction.)

Progress in being assertive: "Alice, I noticed you've left scrap paper and other items on the copier a number of times. Please make a mental note to take them with you when you're done. Thanks."

Your Turn

- My prior "aggressive you" comment:
- My "assertive I" comment:

"Well, I . . ." Examples:

Prior unassertive attempt: "Well, I ... [pauses, looks down at the floor or somewhere else in the room] I think that ... maybe it would be a good idea if perhaps we might ... paint the kitchen a different color."

Progress with assertive attempt: "I would like to have the faded kitchen walls painted a brighter color. Can we pick a time to look at color samples?"

Prior unassertive attempt: "Well, it's only my opinion . . ."

Progress with assertive attempt: [Making direct eye contact] "You may not agree, but I would like you to respect my point of view."

Prior unassertive attempt: "Well, yes, I'll do it."

Progress with assertive attempt: "Thanks for thinking of me, but I am not available at this time." And then change the subject.

Prior unassertive attempt: "Well, I need to go now . . . I really need to go now . . ."

Progress with assertive attempt: "Something has come up

and I'm going to have to end this shortly so I'm going to have to say goodbye for now. Goodbye." And hang up.

✎ Your Turn

- My prior "Well, I" or unassertive comment:
- My "assertive I" comment:

Examples of Phrases to Use and Avoid

Here are examples of words that are likely to elicit a defensive or aggressive reaction, and those that are less likely to do so:

Words likely to elicit a defensive or aggressive reaction	Words less likely to elicit an aggressive reaction
"What you said is wrong!"	"I think there may be more than one explanation for what happened."
"That's not what I said."	"Let me try to express it differently."
"It doesn't work that way."	"Do you think it might work if we tried it another way?"

Feeling Overwhelmed?

How can you keep track of all these aspects of communication while trying to get along with others? You don't have to! Neither you, nor I, nor anyone else can be aware of everything all the time. Remember to take this one step at a time. Maybe you can start by using feeling statements that start with "I." Just start there, try it out, and make adjustments as you go.

As you continue reading this book, you'll learn specific techniques for improving your communication and emotional-coping skills. As we also discussed in Chapter Four, you can only control 50 percent of any conversation: what you say and the way you respond. That also means you are not responsible for the other 50 percent of the discussion.

Like a pebble tossed into a pond, you are changing yourself for the better by using Positive Communication, not going to every argument you are invited to, and practicing more effective emotional-coping skills. This creates a ripple effect where communication will no longer be the same as it was in the past. You are setting in motion changes in your communication style that have the distinct potential to also influence positive change in those around you. So, remember to breathe, take a break now and then from reading, and practice the exercises in this book.

✎ Moving Forward

- List some examples of phrases you'd like to use (and some to avoid) in your interactions with others.

CHAPTER SIX

Listen to Learn—Seek Common Ground

So far, you have reflected on how you communicate, learned how to get your concerns really heard, and examined how you can redirect your energy and concerns in more desirable and effective ways, not necessarily by trying harder, but by trying some things differently.

Arguments also tend to develop and escalate when you assume that you understand another person's viewpoint or intentions. This can lead to an emotional reaction to the misperceptions, with both sides growing increasingly frustrated as the discussion becomes more confusing and difficult to follow. In this chapter, we will now look at how you can prevent, minimize, and often resolve disagreements by practicing more effective listening skills, understanding the other person's point of view, and seeking common ground.

✎ Recall a time when you were talking with someone, and they misunderstood what you were trying to say. How did you feel? Describe the experience in your journal and try to remember that feeling, because that's how others likely feel when you misunderstand them in a conversation. Keeping that in mind can help you catch yourself before you react when someone tells you that you misunderstood them. It can also help you keep an open mind about what the other person might be attempting to communicate.

By contrast, think about how it feels when others accurately hear and respect your opinions, even if they do not entirely agree with you. That feeling can be a powerful motivation to continue practicing more effective listening skills.

Reflecting What You Think You Heard

When you're listening to someone, it can help to respectfully state what you think you are hearing, then ask if you are accurately describing what the other person is saying. If you are unable to state what you think the other person is saying, ask if they can explain it again using different words or examples. Effective communication skills also include catching yourself when very human preconceptions and reactions creep into your thoughts. As a human being, it's easy to project your own worries, fears, and other emotions into your interactions with others. (For example: "Aren't you going to eat more? You must hate my cooking.") Step by step, your insights and confidence will continue to grow while fear and frustration diminish, and you will improve both your listening and communication skills.

Even if the other person does not share your level of commitment to this communication process, improving your listening and communication skills can provide you with additional opportunities to better understand their point of view. You'll also demonstrate your commitment to finding creative solutions to concerns that, in the past, would have probably led to heated stalemates.

Examples

Prior comment: "It seems to be all right when you buy things, but when I buy something, we can't afford it."

Progress: "I think I hear you are concerned about our finances and that we are unable to save money for things we have talked about doing."

- My prior comment, not listening to what someone has said:

- My progress in trying to listen to what someone has said:

Respect Their Emotions

Try to respect the emotions of others, even if you do not understand or agree with what they are feeling or why they feel that way. What someone is feeling at any given moment is what they are feeling; respect that feeling, without judging. Periodically, take a few deep breaths to slow down your heart rate and thought process. Would you be able to consider their concerns more objectively if you didn't have any preconceived opinions about the person sharing those comments? Can you try to listen to the message without getting lost in the emotions?

Examples

Prior comment: "Why are you getting so upset?"

Progress trying to understand what someone is feeling: "I hear that you are upset. Can you help me better understand what you are feeling right now?"

Prior reaction: You tune the other person out as soon as they start raising their voice or sounding angry.

Progress trying to understand what someone is feeling: Catch yourself taking someone else's emotions personally; listen and let the other person vent for several minutes. Then say, "You seem to feel very strongly about this matter. Help me to understand."

✎ Your Turn

- My prior comment at not listening to what someone else is feeling:

- My progress in trying to understand what someone is feeling:

Be Open to Their Viewpoint

Many times, you may find yourself reacting to someone's opinion or suggestion before you've allowed yourself time to think about it. People want to feel heard and understood; reacting before you've even tried to understand where they're coming from not only causes confusion and frustration, but it leads them to feel like their voice doesn't matter to you. One way to stop this reaction is to write down what you think the other person's concerns are, along with any questions you may have. Explain why you are asking questions and make it clear that you want to understand, and therefore be open to, their viewpoint. This can help set the tone for a calmer discussion. And you never know—you may actually agree with them once you listen and make an effort to understand.

Thank the other person for their responses, as this can help both of you to continue more calmly. You can also thank them for clarifying their point of view and being patient with you as you ask questions to help build rapport and credibility in this process. For example: "Thanks for giving me another example of what you meant. I didn't understand some of your concerns at first, but your explanation was very helpful."

Examples

Prior comment reacting to a person's point of view: "Ugh. There's too much going on. You are getting me all confused."

Progress in communicating openness to their point of view: "I may be jotting down some thoughts at times to help me remember what I think you are saying and questions I may need to ask you to help me clear up any misunderstandings.

Prior comment: "You think your way is the only right way!"

Progress: "Could you give me a different example or explanation of what you mean so I can better understand?"

✎ Your Turn

- My prior comment reacting to a person's point of view:

- My progress in communicating openness to hearing their point of view:

Statements such as "You may be right," or "I'm trying to understand the reasons why you want to do this" tend to get someone's attention without making them defensive. Try to avoid deadlines or threats, spoken or unspoken, such as, "If you don't agree on this by the end of the week, just forget all about it," or "If you don't do this, I won't trust you anymore." Acknowledging when you are mistaken in your opinion, impression, or reaction helps build trust, and demonstrates the value of ongoing discussions: "I guess I can get defensive at times and miss some of the points you try to make." Sharing what you think without contradicting the other person allows everyone to save face.[14]

Dealing with Silence

Pauses in conversations may be uncomfortable for a while, but they can actually serve a constructive purpose. It's OK to be quiet and think, with your mind open and your mouth closed (instead of the other way around). Taking time to think about someone else's question or comment, or what you want to say next, can help turn periods of silence into normal and positive occurrences. With time, you can grow more comfortable with these periods of silence. My experience is that many people continue to dislike them but become better able to tolerate them.

When you need a period of silence, briefly state your reason constructively, rather than giving a defensive response, such as "I am thinking—is that a problem for you?" Instead, you might say something like, "I'm just taking a moment to think about that so I can give you a clear response."

Negotiating

The authors of *Getting to Yes* (who also founded the Program on Negotiation at Harvard Law School) describe negotiating as "the process of communicating back and forth for the purpose of reaching a joint decision."[15] They point out that it's easy to sometimes forget that a negotiation is not a debate; consequently, your competitive urges can start to creep into the negotiation process. Competition serves us well in some areas of life, but it can complicate problem-solving communication.

Try to approach negotiations with a win-win proposition (where you both gain something) instead of a win-lose (where someone has to win and the other must lose). Can you agree on an outcome that isn't ideal for either of you, recognizing that the ongoing, working relationship is more important? Instead of meeting someone halfway (fifty-fifty), try to match your 55 percent effort to their 45 percent. Most likely, each person thinks they are giving more than 50 percent of the effort. Make the extra effort yourself and continue to move forward.

Don't make the mistake of routinely going to 70 percent, 80 percent, or even more, where you're offering much more than the other party. In any type of relationship, this often leads to an unhealthy and counterproductive situation for both parties. Try to catch yourself if you have the tendency to give in just for the sake of peace. Agreeing or compromising just to end an argument tends to build resentment, which can damage relationships and lead to even more heated arguments in the future.

Seek and build upon your common ground, and periodically review your points of agreement together or individually, if needed. During arguments, people tend to focus on areas of disagreement, which usually increases defensiveness and leads to even more disagreement. Your memories of past arguments, accurate or not, may also resurface. "Oh yeah, well, six months ago, you said you would fix the sink, and it still drips . . . and ten years ago, you said you hated my mother!"

When you focus on finding points of agreement, however small they may initially seem, you are likely to identify one or more and build upon them. This simple shift in focus can pave a smoother road to solutions that make both of you happy. According to Gregorio Billikopf, a Labor Management Farm Advisor for the University of California, Davis, "Agreement becomes much easier if both parties feel ownership of the ideas . . . A proposal evolves that bears enough of the suggestions of both sides for each to feel it is theirs."[16]

Sample Negotiation

Pete and Mary have not gone away on a vacation since they decided to start a family. Now that their two children no longer need diapers, these parents have been talking about taking a much-needed vacation. Pete enjoys the outdoors and would like to go camping; Mary does not. In the past, this would have probably resulted in a heated argument, with hurt feelings, increased stress, and much frustration. However, this time, before emotions could escalate, they called a time-out and agreed to talk again after the children had gone to bed. Instead of listing reasons why camping would be such a great idea, Pete decides to ask Mary what her concerns are about this type of vacation.

Expecting another argument, Mary initially reacts defensively, raising her voice and stating that she wants to go on a real vacation. Pete catches himself and deflects the comments without taking them personally. He thanks her for her willingness to talk about this again and asks her to help him understand her concerns about going camping. This seems to get Mary's attention and shows her that perhaps her husband really wants to understand her concerns and what she means by a "real" vacation.

As Pete tries to listen to Mary's concerns instead of thinking about how he'll justify his desire to go camping, he hears:

- While camping would save money, it would involve a lot of work for her, being that the children are still quite young. In addition to packing clothes for herself and the children, she would also need to pack toys and cooking utensils. That does not sound restful to her.

- The last time they went camping (before children), there was a thunderstorm while they were putting up the tent. The thought of that happening again with young children made her want to scream. To her credit, she did not.

- Mary's idea of a vacation is having a real bed to sleep in.

Pete repeats what he thinks he heard Mary say were her concerns about camping with small children. She replies, "Yes, and . . ." at which point Pete begins to interrupt her. This time he catches himself later than he did a few moments ago, but before he or Mary escalates the discussion into a heated argument. Although he is disappointed that Mary does not want to go camping, he apologizes for being impatient and interrupting her. He tells her, "Please continue with what you were going to say." They agree to think about other options, such as finding a motel or similar accommodation near a lake, and to continue discussing this over the next two weeks.

Several days later during a lunch break, Pete mentions the disagreement to Charlie, a friend and coworker. Charlie tells him about a family camp he and his family have been visiting for the past few summers. Later that evening, Pete tries to build upon Mary's desire to go on vacation "with a real bed to sleep on" and no meals to prepare. He begins to tell her about the place Charlie and his family have been going to. Besides coinciding with Pete's desire to be closer to nature, this place has individual cabins for each family and provides family-style meals.

Mary is leery about this option but agrees to check out the family camp's website to learn more about it. While many of the photos appear quite enticing, she still has concerns. Pete offers to write down all her concerns and discuss them with Charlie, whom Mary knows and likes. If she still is not interested in pursuing this option, he agrees to consider other ideas instead. He also offers to help with packing clothes and toys for the children regardless of which option they agree on for their vacation. These last two comments help Mary feel her concerns are really being heard and increase her willingness to explore this option.

Mary wants to know more about the cabins, what they look like inside, whether they have electricity, and whether there are flush toilets and showers. Pete writes down each of her concerns, as well as some of his own questions. Since the camp is on a lake, is there a designated swim area with a lifeguard? What other activities are there for kids and parents? Pete meets again with Charlie, who answers each of their questions. Mary is glad to hear that every cabin and building has electricity. Pete tells her the bathrooms and showers have hot and cold running water, but they are in separate buildings, a short distance from the cabins. Mary would rather have the comfort of a bathroom in their own cabin.

Pete explains that one of the reasons he enjoys camping is the peacefulness that not having a TV or other electronic devices gives him. He is learning that explaining his concerns in a positive and respectful manner before he presents additional ideas or opinions increases the likelihood of his wife listening and understanding him. He also recognizes that trying to build upon one of his wife's ideas with some of his own can turn a past obstacle into a new opportunity to move forward together.[17]

There are no TVs or Wi-Fi in the cabins, and due to the camp's remote setting, phone calls are limited to payphones. This suits Pete, and Mary is not troubled about the lack of connectivity, provided there are other interests she can pursue while there. Though neither has gotten their ideal choice of a vacation spot, they agree there are many things that interest each of them about this particular experience. Mary and Pete decide to finalize plans to spend one week at the family camp. They also agree that, regardless of how this vacation turns out, they are pleased with how they have worked together to reach this decision.

Turn Stalemates into Opportunities

When two or more people come to a stalemate in which no further agreement appears possible, brainstorming—or rapidly stating ideas out loud—can often get each person's creative skills and imagination stimulated, providing an opportunity to move forward together. Brainstorming can be an invaluable tool for helping couples, parents, children, roommates, coworkers, and even our elected officials consider new possibilities.

When brainstorming, record every alternative that's generated, without initially commenting for or against any ideas, no matter how far-fetched some may seem.

Brainstorming Example

Lara and her husband Fred have been trying to reach some agreement on how to manage their finances. They decide to try brainstorming to come up with one or more ideas that they can agree on. Fred writes down every idea, without comment, on sheets of paper as fast as he can without concern for spelling or neatness. The point is to capture ideas quickly and keep the process moving.

Both Fred and Lara shout out ideas. They do this for several minutes with ideas coming thick and fast, then for another few minutes as ideas come more slowly. Afterward, Lara tapes their list on a wall.

Here's what they came up with:

- Create a budget and stick to it
- Spend less money
- Prioritize better
- Cut back on unnecessary purchases
- Play lottery
- Win lottery

- Consolidate credit cards
- Get rid of credit cards
- For one or more months record every purchase to see where $ goes
- Seek out lower interest credit card and when paid off, pay new bill in full at end of month to eliminate monthly fees
- Hope some long-lost relative dies and leaves us a fortune

Lara ranks what she thinks are the five most desirable, realistic options, with #1 being most desirable:

1. Spend less $
2. Create a budget and stick to it
3. Seek out lower interest credit card and when paid off, pay new bill in full at end of month to eliminate monthly fees
4. Consolidate credit cards
5. Cut back on unnecessary purchases

Fred then ranks or prioritizes what he thinks are the five most desirable or realistic options:

1. Prioritize better
2. Seek out lower interest credit card and when paid off, pay new bill in full at end of month to eliminate monthly fees
3. For one or more months record every purchase to see where $ goes
4. Create a budget and stick to it
5. Get rid of credit cards

As we can see from their lists, Lara and Fred do not rank any of the options in the exact same way. One way to approach their differences in opinion is to discuss the pros and cons of each prioritized idea. In trying to focus on what they do agree on, they are able to acknowledge that they are both concerned about their finances. As they look at the ideas generated by the brainstorming session, they agree on the following:

1. They both want to reduce their expenses.

2. They compromise and agree to seek out a lower-interest credit card, as it is a high priority for both of them, even though it's not the number-one priority for either. Fred offers to search online for credit card offers.

3. They will prioritize paying off credit card debt due to the high interest payments.

Looking again at their list of ideas, they see that the number-one priority for Lara—to spend less money—is quite similar to Fred's, which is to prioritize better.

They agree to discuss on another day how their money is spent using their checkbook, credit card statements, and other receipts for reference. They also agree to save the list for future discussion in case some ideas appear more desirable or practical later, or, when combined with another idea, may inspire new ones.

Sleep On It

Many people feel better if they wait until the next day to act upon an important decision, such as making a major purchase or accepting a new job. Looking back at your own experiences, how many times have you thought you just had to have or do something, only to find that a day or two later the desire was less intense? Whenever possible, try waiting at least a day before following through on a major decision. This allows you time to reconsider the pros and cons of the action so you can see more clearly whether you're making a sound decision, or if perhaps your idea needs some fine-tuning.

If you're struggling to agree on an important decision with another person, can you agree that you disagree and reschedule further discussions for another time? After giving an issue a chance to cool down, one or more parties might find a new perspective. Continuing the discussion at a later time can also reduce the pressure to force or rush a decision.

Of course, some decisions cannot be postponed. A car will not start and is needed for transportation to work, a child-care provider is ill, or a parent or guardian has surgery and cannot work for a while—no matter how proactive you try to be, life just happens sometimes.

Live, and Let Live

Ongoing disagreements may also involve significant differences of opinion over certain philosophical, political, or spiritual/religious beliefs. Some differences of opinion are not always resolved to everyone's complete satisfaction. In recognizing the many other positive qualities in each other, many differences can be managed, respected, or at least tolerated. For example, when two parents are of different religious or spiritual beliefs, many agree to raise their children in more than one faith, providing the children with a foundation and support to build on and incorporate into their own belief system when they reach adulthood. Spouses and friends can agree to not discuss certain political issues while continuing to enjoy each other's company. You can live with your beliefs and convictions and allow others to live with theirs if you can find common ground.

In an ideal world, we would always accept each other as individuals and fully embrace our differences with an open mind. I won't pretend to know how to accomplish this, nor do I possess the ability to consistently apply this in my own life. I do not have all the answers to all of life's challenges, but fortunately, I do not have to take that burden upon my all-too-human shoulders. What you and I can both do is keep learning to the best of our abilities.

✐ Moving Forward

- What is one issue that you would like to resolve by brainstorming with someone else? After taking a few moments to reflect on why resolving that issue is important to you, reach out to the other person involved (perhaps a spouse, friend, or coworker) and schedule a brainstorming session.

CHAPTER SEVEN

You Don't Have to Keep Arguing with Yourself

Reader discretion advised: some of the following may expose you to examples of internal communication that closely resemble your own. Someone once said, "It takes a lot of energy to carry a grudge, hold onto resentments, jump to conclusions . . ." and wrestle with excessive guilt. When you take responsibility for your own actions and emotions, regardless of what someone else does or doesn't do, you'll feel better about yourself. It also frees up precious time and energy that you might otherwise expend continuing to justify past actions or worrying about the future. By letting go, you'll empower yourself to move forward.

Holding on to the Past

The word "resentment" comes from the Latin *re,* meaning "again," and *sentire,* meaning "to feel." When you hold onto resentment, you continue to "feel again" or "re-feel" the original pain. If you felt hurt, offended, angry, or embarrassed, and you continue to re-feel the same thing over and over again, will you feel any better? Even if everyone you know agrees that you didn't deserve what happened, holding onto those thoughts will just make you re-feel those unpleasant feelings indefinitely.

To top it all off, the person whose words or actions hurt you may not even be aware of the effect they had, or even remember what happened. Resentments, unresolved guilt, and other bottled-up emotions can provide fuel for future arguments and distract you from current issues. In this chapter, you'll have a chance to explore your internal conversations and look at how you can lessen the enormous energy drain and distress they cause.

I vividly remember one of the first family support meetings I attended many years ago. An older woman was sharing her strength, hope, and experience living with an alcoholic husband. She said, "For the sake of argument, let us say that all of our problems were someone else's fault. By getting help and support, we don't have to wait for the other person to change in order for us to feel better."

That really got my attention. I hadn't realized that it was possible to *not* get angry when someone spoke to me harshly. I couldn't understand how a person wouldn't feel hurt when someone close to them was being overly critical. I remember that I was tired of waiting for others to change so I could feel better. I also remember the facial expressions of the people at that meeting, and the tone of their voices. Through those cues, they strongly communicated to me that something was indeed working for them. Many of those present that evening didn't seem to be filled with the anger and pain that was filling me. When I heard each of them share, I knew that they understood what I was feeling, even though I hadn't uttered one word.

A dear friend of mine, John Holden, who lived to the ripe old age of ninety-seven, passed these brief words of wisdom to me: "Beware of self-righteous indignation." *Who, me? I've got a right to be angry.*

If you find yourself justifying why you stay angry, it may be helpful to repeat John's words or a similar phrase to yourself. Nowhere have I ever read that you should like being treated or spoken to unfairly. However, when you hold on to resentments, self-righteous indignation, or other uncomfortable emotions, you tie yourself to the past and continue to re-experience those undesirable feelings. But when you let go of past resentments, you free yourself of that pain and discomfort. As author John E. Southard has said, "The only people with whom you should try to get even with are those who have helped you."

Tip-Of-The-Iceberg Reactions

Although you might think you know the reason behind your strong feelings of anger, sadness, or other emotions, those feelings are often like an iceberg—there's much more to them than meets the eye. It is estimated that 90 percent of an iceberg lies beneath the surface of the water, out of sight. Sometimes a conversation or disagreement can trigger powerful memories that lie beneath the surface of your awareness or consciousness. One comment can trigger past memories, even if not directly related to the matter at hand. Maybe you're reminded subconsciously of when you were bullied as a child, or a past romantic relationship that did not end well. Recognizing that other issues can intrude into your current relationships might help you use the tools you've acquired to minimize disruptive effects so you can continue to learn and grow.

When you overreact to an issue that's just the tip of the iceberg, you can try to apologize and use respectful communication to deal with one issue at a time, rather than letting past issues collide with present concerns. If needed, call a time-out and walk away until you can regain your composure. However, repeated overreactions, especially those that turn violent or temporarily overwhelm an individual, suggest other potential concerns, such as clinical depression, panic attacks associated with an anxiety disorder, post-traumatic stress, a chemical imbalance, or other factors that may require more help or a medical diagnosis. We will discuss these in Chapter Ten, *What To Do When You Need More Help.*

You do not have to do this alone. There is help, and there is hope!

Reward Positive Actions

Rewarding the positive actions of loved ones, students, and employees is more likely to influence healthy and constructive choices than nags or threats ever could. If you catch someone you care about doing something right, thoughtful, kind, or considerate, acknowledge it with a simple "thank you," "nice job," or, "I appreciate your taking the time to do that." Tangible reinforcements or rewards—such as preparing a favorite meal or dessert, going out for ice cream or a movie, or doing something else they like to do—can also encourage those desirable behaviors to continue. Remind yourself how you feel when someone speaks to you encouragingly, even when the comment suggests that a change in certain behaviors might be in order. This is not a matter of being too easy on someone, or being afraid to hurt someone's feelings; instead, you're encouraging the positive change that will benefit you both.

Try to make a point of saying something nice about the other person in your life each day. When you were first dating, making a new friend, or when your first child was very young, you probably did this often. This is because during the honeymoon phase of romantic relationships, endorphins, the "feel-good" chemicals, are triggered in the reward centers of the brain. This is thought to play a vital part in human reproductive survival. [18]

According to researchers, friendships also activate the reward centers of the brain, and can have a significant positive effect on longevity. [19] [20] In time, these reward centers become less active, and the responsibilities and challenges of life can easily distract you from acknowledging the positive qualities in those very people who are most important to you. Fortunately, you can relearn the habit of acknowledging others. You don't have to sit and wait for someone else to do it!

Catch a Loved One (and Yourself) Doing Something Positive

In addition to expressing your concerns, try to periodically (and without overkill) praise and reward the positive decisions and healthy behaviors of your loved ones, friends, coworkers, and employees. And finally, don't forget about yourself: as you continue to model self-caring behavior, periodically remind yourself of the many caring, healthy, and otherwise constructive decisions you make every day—yes, every day! If you sat down and made a list of the positive choices you make in any given day, they'd probably well outnumber the things you wish you could do over.

✐ Actually, can you take a few moments to do that now? Think back on the last 24 hours. In your journal, brainstorm and record all positive decisions you have made, whether they concern health and safety or being respectful, organized, or proactive. Write your list without second-guessing yourself, and as quickly as the thoughts come. Take a few moments now and later to reflect on your list of positive decisions and actions.

If you could be fully aware of all the positive decisions your loved ones (or roommates, friends, coworkers) make every day, how much would it help balance your perceptions of their less-than-desirable actions or comments?

✐ Record the name of one of these people in your journal and list all the positive comments or actions they have made over the past several days. Take a few moments now and later to reflect on your list.

Stop Enabling Undesirable Behaviors

Do the following complaints sound familiar?

- "I am sick and tired of cleaning up after everyone else's mess!"
- "Things had better change around here and change fast!"
- "I work so hard at my job and when I get home all I hear is *'Honey, do this'* or *'Dad, I need you to do this.'* It seems everyone is always looking for me to do something for them!"

When I hear comments like these, I have often asked my clients, "Who are you really angry with?" Frequently, the response is, "I'm angry with myself for doing things that others can and need to do for themselves." When you repeatedly do for others what they can and ought to do for themselves, who benefits? Who really gets help?

Not only does it often cause you to neglect your own needs or responsibilities, but it robs the other person of opportunities to practice necessary life or job skills, as well as the self-confidence and self-respect they would gain in the process. Even if you think you have the other person's best interests at heart, your actions may communicate that you do not have faith in their ability to do things for themselves.

At times, it may seem quicker or less of a hassle to just do certain things yourself, or try to fix the mistakes of a loved one, friend, or coworker; but over time, this can develop into a pattern that contributes to future problems and arguments.

By doing what someone else can and should do for themselves, you make it easier for them to continue with the undesirable behavior. They may even know how to get you to meet their responsibilities by trying to make you feel guilty, arguing to wear you down, or not performing to your satisfaction. In the long run, the urge to over-protect or fix another person's problems often has the opposite effect: they'll be even less confident or less motivated to deal with challenges in the future. Smaller problems that aren't dealt with now can develop into bigger problems later. While you can continue to provide encouragement, love, and emotional support, there is no doubt that self-confidence and competence come from doing, and even making mistakes along the way. Self-confidence and competence cannot be given to anyone.

By allowing others to experience the natural consequences of their actions (within reason), you demonstrate your confidence that they can learn and grow as individuals. Sometimes the hardest thing to say to someone you care about is, "No, I cannot do this for you," even when the most loving and supportive thing you might say is, "I love you [or care about you], but you need to learn how to do this." Continue to model healthy, self-caring, boundary-setting behaviors—both physically and emotionally—and fewer self-neglecting behaviors.

After using positive and respectful approaches to communicate desired changes and your rationale for them, there may come a time when it is appropriate and necessary to allow others to experience the natural consequences of their actions.

Examples of Allowing Others to Experience Natural Consequences

Prior attempt: "You should call me if you are going to be

late coming home instead of just showing up and making me worried sick."

Progress: "I get really worried when you're late coming home and I don't know where you are. I'd appreciate it if you would call or text me to let me know if you're going to be more than twenty minutes late. Thanks."

Allowing others to experience natural consequences: "As I've mentioned before, I get really worried when you're late coming home and I don't know where you are. I'd appreciate it if you would call or text me to let me know if you are going to be more than twenty minutes late. [I love you and] I enjoy sharing meals together, but if you are late for supper and have not called or texted, I will leave a place setting on the table and put the leftovers in the fridge for you to heat up when you get home." Then, when your loved one or roommate comes home, try to be brief and as courteous as possible by greeting them, and let them know that supper is in the refrigerator for them to reheat.

Allowing others to experience natural consequences [to teen]: "As I've mentioned before, I get really worried when you're late coming home and I don't know where you are. I'd appreciate it if you would call or text me to let me know if you are going to be more than a few minutes late. Because you're over twenty minutes late with no word from you, this is the consequence [e.g., earlier curfew for a set period]."

Prior complaint: "I am sick and tired of having to pick up after you all the time. I am not your maid! How much effort does it take to put your dirty clothes where they belong?"

Progress: "You forgot to put the soiled clothes in the hamper. Can you please do that now so it will be done with?"

Allowing others to experience natural consequences: "I'll be doing the laundry on Saturday. Please remember to put whatever you want to be cleaned in the hamper. Any clothes not in the hamper will not get washed, so you will need to wash them yourself. Thanks."

Allowing others to experience natural consequences [to coworker]: "I want to be supportive, but I also need to meet the responsibilities of my own job. You will need to finish this."

When you decide to communicate positively and respectfully, and to no longer take on certain responsibilities for others, try to be as consistent as possible. If you follow through on your intentions three times out of four, the other person is likely to remember the one time you gave in, and might use it as an excuse to resume the undesirable behavior. When people are used to having another person do things for them, they often resist change, whether they truly forget, pretend to forget, or actively resist.

Similar to calling a time-out, physically moving away from the room with the dirty laundry can help you keep or regain your composure and, at times, your sanity. So, what happens if you mess up and give in? You would not be the first person (or the millionth) to do so. It could be AFGE, another freakin' growth experience. Try to learn from it as best you can and build upon the experience. Over time, there will be fewer of these occurrences.

I once saw an anonymous quote: "Good judgment comes from experience, and experience comes from poor judgment." Try to remember—relationships are challenging for all of us! It will take time for you to acquire additional communication and coping tools and to gain experience using them. It will take time for others as well. Repeating phrases to yourself such as "Let it go" or "I can only change myself" can redirect your thoughts away from what others are doing (or not doing), and help you focus on moving forward.

Remember to use your own good judgment when choosing to let others accept the responsibilities of their own actions. In addition to adapting this approach to the circumstances and your knowledge of the other person, you need to consider the issue of immediate safety. If someone has fallen and appears to have hurt themselves, helping them is the compassionate and appropriate action to take.

Let Go of Anger and Resentment

As much as you may try to be proactive, calm, and objective in your interactions with others, there will still be times when you get really ticked off. You are not alone!

Hopefully, you or the other person will call a time-out and put some physical distance between you. But even with the distance, you might still be fuming. While you may be tempted to slam doors or kitchen cabinets, such actions are counter-productive and do more harm than good. Experience also tells us that trying to show people what they look like by giving them a "taste of their own medicine" is seldom effective. Instead of getting the desired response of, "I see what you are doing. You are acting that way to help me see how rude I was by talking to you the same way," you're more likely to hear, "Why are you acting like such a jerk?!"

Letting go of anger takes time and practice, but you probably already knew that. Many of us have spent quite some time dwelling on what others have said, done, or not done. You may have developed strong patterns in which you've reinforced this type of thinking through rationalization, blame, self-righteous indignation, or repetition. Over time, you can create healthier patterns of communication through positive self-talk and by paying better attention to your own needs. In this way, you can learn to better cope with your own emotions. From time to time, review the notes you have made on mnemonic devices or other additional insights you have gained. Practice them and you'll see how they can help you let go of or reduce your anger and resentment.

Rewarding yourself for the positive changes you're making will not only reinforce that progress, but will also bolster hope and encouragement so you can weather more difficult times. As a human being, it's important to not only take care of your physical needs, but also your emotional and mental health.

Let Go of Excessive Guilt

You know that nagging feeling you get when something deep inside you says, "I wish I had stopped and taken a few deep breaths before I opened my mouth in anger," or, "I knew I was feeling very tired when I came home and overreacted to what Jennifer said"? Apologizing can be uncomfortable. It may even seem easier to ignore that feeling and forget about it, but emotions have a pesky way of building up over time, and you'll use more energy in the long run when you continue to rationalize your avoidance of what you know you need to do. Repressed emotions will usually come out in other ways. It may be in trying to find fault in others: "See, I am not the only one who messes up around here." Or, maybe you turn to food, alcohol, gambling, or some other unhealthy behavior to avoid dealing with your feelings.

When you're determined to wait for the other person to apologize first, it can feel like you're stuck in a silent argument raging inside your head and, at times, your stomach. How much time and energy do you waste waiting for the other person to change first? When you have said or done something you regret, it's in your own best interest to apologize, because it will lessen your feelings of guilt and remorse while increasing your self-respect. Earlier, we discussed the benefits of KISS: Keep It Simple, Sweetheart. Keeping this expression in mind can help you to apologize more quickly.

Also remember that you can only control 50 percent of a conversation. If the other person accepts your apology, that's a bonus, but not a requirement. I suggest not waiting for a "thank you," or for the other person to accept the apology, as it may take time for them to process it and work through their own emotions. Even when they genuinely believe in the sincerity of the apology, it can still take time for them to heal from the perceived hurt and work through their own emotions.

Alexander Pope said, "A man should never be ashamed to own he has been in the wrong, which is but saying, in other words, that he is wiser than he was yesterday." Yet, societal pressures can make it especially uncomfortable for men to apologize, as many men fear they'll be perceived as weak. Of course, the reality is that men are just as biologically and psychologically capable of expressing emotions and initiating apologies as women—and need to do so every bit as much. It can begin with something as basic as, "I am sorry for the other day." It's not always necessary to admit you were wrong. If you cannot get those words out of your mouth, begin with whatever you can, even if it's "I'm sorry that happened," or "I wish I had put my brain in gear before I opened my mouth." Some people apologize by putting themselves down: "I am such a jerk," "I can be such an idiot sometimes," or even harsher comments. If that is your pattern, this may be an opportunity to try something different. Putting yourself down might temporarily lessen some of the guilt you feel, but can often make it more difficult to apologize in the future.

Some of us have developed a habit of saying "I'm sorry" as a courtesy when "Excuse me," "I didn't realize this seat was taken," or other clarifying comments might be more suitable. Apologizing for actions that were not your fault can develop into a pattern of unnecessary guilt and could also reduce credibility when you really do need to apologize. Harold Kushner, in *When Bad Things Happen to Good People*, states, "An appropriate sense of guilt makes people try to be better. But an excessive sense of guilt . . . robs us of our self-esteem and perhaps our capacity to grow and act."[21] Too much guilt or negative self-talk can consume precious time and energy and divert your attention from things you can actually control.

Trying to be respectful to others and to yourself one day at a time can do wonders in the long run to lessen excessive feelings of guilt. As you continue to learn and grow, your actions will demonstrate your growth more than your words.

Projecting Into the Future

When you project your anger, guilt, worries, and insecurities onto another human being or into the future, these feelings tend to grow larger and stronger. Imagine you are sitting in a movie theater: What happens to the size of the picture as it is projected onto the screen in front of you? It becomes many, many times larger!

One example of projecting is when you carry on a dialogue in your mind as if you were having an actual conversation with another person:

"I am not going to apologize to Juan because he will just say that he knew I was wrong. Then I will tell him that at least I am honest enough to apologize when I am wrong, but that he's too stubborn to admit his own mistakes. Then he will start raising his voice like he always does and bring up comments about my weight. Who does he think he is, Mister Perfect? I try so hard to provide a good home and be a good spouse, and all I ever get is criticism. He will go on and on about how I don't get around to vacuuming often enough. Why doesn't he get off his lazy rear end and do more around the house? It does no good to try to talk to him. All I ever hear is criticism. I am so sick of it. The next time he does something wrong, he is really going to hear it from me!"

Like the example with Juan's spouse, projecting your own thoughts and emotions onto someone else's motives often fuels increasingly strong internal reactions. Catching yourself earlier will save you a great deal of time and energy. Mnemonic devices and concise phrases can be particularly helpful in these situations. Repeating "Slow down" or "Let it go" can truly help slow down and redirect such thoughts. With continued practice, you'll find yourself thinking things like: "If this were a few months ago, I would have let this issue fester in my mind for hours or maybe even days," or, "There I go again, projecting the worst before she gets home. I am recognizing this pattern more often before I say something I might regret."

Try Not to Take It Personally

Trying not to take things personally can be particularly difficult, even when you catch yourself and remember it is in your own best interest to be proactive instead of reactive. A loved one, friend, or coworker may be angry or upset about something else and, on occasion, appear to take it out on you through a harsh tone or a critical comment.

Picture a frazzled mother with three screaming kids who are having a meltdown in the middle of a store. If she were to sound irritable, agitated, or annoyed, would you immediately assume that her comments were pointed at you personally? You would probably recognize, due to the physical signs or cues, that her manner was the result of the distressing situation around her, independent of you or anyone else. With practice, you can learn to listen more objectively to what is really going on with others instead of reacting defensively or critically. As we discussed in Chapter Three, if you want to know what someone else is thinking or feeling, you can ask them respectfully, at a time when your question is most likely to be received objectively and less defensively.

If a friend or loved one struggles with a major mental health disorder or addiction, it can help to visualize the person with a bandage wrapped around their head, because these are brain diseases, after all. With help and support, you can continue to love the individual, even while you hate their disease. We will discuss this in more detail in Chapter Ten, *What To Do When You Need More Help.*

When you see a pile of dirty dishes in the sink and start to feel a rising sense of irritation, take a deep breath and try to remember that sometimes dirty dishes are just dirty dishes, not a reflection of how your partner or someone else values you. Each one of us is a work in progress; we make mistakes and learn from them—but sometimes we are aggravatingly slow to learn. Comments such as, "If you loved me, you wouldn't . . ." or, "If you would just get off your lazy butt once in a while and do your share of the work" often fuel arguments, and no longer need to be part of your conversations.

Try to catch yourself when you react or feel like saying, "I just told you what I was going to do," or "Weren't you listening to what I just said?" Consider that the other person may have been distracted, and respond with, "Perhaps I could have expressed my plans better—what I meant to say was . . ." Remembering that someone else's actions are their responsibility and not yours can also help you to catch yourself. For parents, remember it is your responsibility to help and nurture your children and teens to the best of your abilities, but being able to control their behavior is a myth.

Sometimes the best way to show someone you care about them is to simply let them feel angry, annoyed, sad, or just have a bad day, without taking it personally or feeling the need to fix things when they don't want you to. You don't have to like the other person's mood, but you can let them know you care and that you're available whenever they want to talk.

Try to Put Yourself in Someone Else's Shoes

I remember being taught as a child, "Now, little Jerry, try to put yourself in Joey's shoes. How do you think he feels when you won't share with him? How do you feel when someone will not share with you?" Trying to put yourself in someone else's place can help you develop sensitivity. It's one of many important social skills that can help you work and live with others, but there are still some limitations to this approach.

When my first child was born, I became a stay-at-home dad for two years. It was one of the best decisions I have ever made—except for the time I gave my infant daughter a bath with Ivory Snow laundry detergent instead of Ivory hand soap. Both boxes had a picture of a cute baby and . . . *OK, I messed up.* She survived with only a mild rash and today is a successful professional in her own right. Anyway, I could say to a young mother that I've been a stay-at-home father and can relate to some of her concerns—but that was a long time ago, so some of my recollections may not be completely accurate. More importantly, I can relate as a father but not as a mother, no matter how similar our experiences might have been. As much as I might try to relate to her, at some point, I would be projecting my male feelings, experiences, and biases into the conversation. This doesn't necessarily make my emotions, insights, or experiences invalid; but even if I were relating with another stay-at-home father, I cannot entirely know how another individual thinks and feels, even if I truly have the best of intentions to understand and support them by putting myself in their shoes. This can be a valid and worthwhile exercise, provided I acknowledge that, at best, it's a guess about what another person might feel.

To find out how they really feel, you can ask the other person, when appropriate, how they are feeling or what they are thinking. Remember to keep it simple! "I remember how challenging it was being a parent of small children. How are things going?" Empathetic statements such as, "You seem tired. Do you feel all right?" or "I'm impressed with how you hold down a full-time job and take care of two children" can help communicate your concern and elicit a response.

Nature Abhors a Vacuum

Replacing undesirable thoughts and emotions with healthier ones can help you create positive changes and make you less likely to slip back into old patterns. Earlier, I mentioned the sound that occurs when you open a new jar of pickles and the air rushes in to replace the air that was removed during the canning process. When you work to reduce undesirable actions and patterns of thinking, the old patterns may come rushing back in, sometimes without notice. When you're trying to let go of resentment, it can be helpful to replace those feelings with compassion.

OK, if you are unable to feel compassion at this time or even consider the idea, what might you replace it with?

Examples:

"I can replace feelings of resentment with some healthy self-care today."

"I can replace excessive guilt with positive self-talk about the progress I'm making."

Review the previous chapters or your notes in your journal for additional ideas.

Enter your responses in your journal.

✐ Moving Forward

Think about some of the ways you might replace your undesirable feelings with feelings of compassion, or with more positive actions.

- I can try to replace resentment with . . .
- I can try to replace anger with . . .
- I can try to replace excessive guilt with . . .
- I can try to replace . . . with . . .

CHAPTER EIGHT

Practice Makes Progress

When my father was diagnosed with prostate cancer in his mid-seventies, I drove him to one of his radiation treatments at Bassett Hospital in bucolic Cooperstown in upstate New York. To many people, Cooperstown is best known as the home of the Baseball Hall of Fame.

His doctors told him that, due to the late-onset and type of prostate cancer he had, he would not die from it. He lived many more years, and his cancer never spread beyond the original tumor. The hospital was a one-and-a-half-hour drive from his home in the little town of Downsville, New York, near the dam of the Pepacton Reservoir, which serves far-away New York City. After driving for approximately forty-five minutes through small towns, up and down steep grades, and along winding roads, we came to a crossroads. My father instructed me to slow down, as he wanted to tell me which way to turn. When I told him that I knew which way to go, he responded in a surprised tone, "Do you know how to get to Cooperstown?" I said, "Yes—practice, practice, practice" (referring to the Hall of Fame). We both had a good laugh, which helped break some of the tension from the reason for the trip.

But practice isn't just for aspiring athletes—transforming what you learn into effective communication skills takes repeated practice over time. With patience and persistence, you'll be able to develop and practice healthier emotional coping skills. These coping skills will help you catch yourself when you remember that "practice makes progress" in your interactions with others, and also help you set more realistic goals. You will have more opportunities to acquire more tools and practice preparing for emotionally charged situations later in this chapter. Remember that you deserve to use positive and respectful communication with yourself, as well.

Warning Signs: HALT and SOS

These mnemonics stand for "Hungry, Angry, Lonely, Tired" (HALT) and "Stressed Out Severely" (SOS), and they can function as safety valves. How good are you at taking care of yourself? Are you more reactive in taking care of your own needs by putting others first, instead of being proactive and taking adequate care of yourself? The old saying, "An ounce of prevention is worth a pound of cure" not only applies to your physical, emotional, and mental well-being, but also to your relationships with others. In calmer moments, it's helpful to reflect on those times when smaller everyday irritations—like how others load the dishwasher or squeeze the toothpaste tube—seem to bother you more at certain times. Rome may not have been built in a day, but when I am overly tired, I can build mountains out of molehills in minutes.

Remembering HALT and SOS can shed light on whether an issue with another person is truly significant, or simply a warning sign that you need to slow down, look inwards, and meet one or more of your own needs.

Self-Care Is Not Being Selfish

If you have ever flown on a commercial airline, you probably recall some of the instructions the flight attendant gave before the plane took off. For example, you're told to put on your own oxygen mask before assisting others, even if you are with a young child or infant. This makes sense, because if you pass out from lack of oxygen, how can you help the child?

But in everyday life, the mere thought of putting your

personal well-being before that of your child can result in an emotional tug-of-war with yourself. Many of us were taught as children to put others first, and that putting ourselves first was selfish. You may still believe this and yet, at times, feel unappreciated by family or certain friends "for all the things you do for them," and then feel additional guilt for having these thoughts and feelings.

Taking care of yourself is not being selfish; selfishness is always putting yourself first, and rarely doing anything for others. Taking care of yourself is self-preservation, the natural instinct of all living organisms. Self-care and self-preservation mean: "I come first so that I may maintain adequate physical, emotional, and mental health in order to live and help others." When you neglect one or more of these needs over time, what happens to the way you interact with loved ones? Who benefits from your self-neglect? Not you, and certainly not your spouse, children, coworkers , or your other close relationships. When I am overly hungry, angry, lonely, tired, or stressed out severely, I usually don't like being around myself either! More often than not, it is those closest to me who eventually bear the brunt of my impatience and frustration. When you neglect any of those physical needs for too long, your body will try to get your attention, in usually unpleasant ways. How can you continue to care for your significant relationships if you are not taking adequate care of yourself?

Prioritizing and Managing Time

Does it feel like you never have enough time to do all the things you want or need to do? The to-do lists many of us jot down or keep in our heads never seem to end. I know of no magic answers or secret tricks to find more hours in the day, but I do know this: developing, adapting, or building upon an existing system that helps you plan and prioritize will help you reduce stress and be more successful over time.

Getting more organized begins with small steps. Choose one concern or stressor and break it down into more manageable chunks or objectives. Reminders such as "first things first" can help you prioritize tasks in order of importance, deadlines, or other factors, such as the weather (like when you're deciding to tackle indoor versus outdoor chores). Other reminders, like telling yourself to slow down, can help you pace yourself physically, mentally, or emotionally. Do you have a relative, friend, coworker, or supervisor who seems well organized and able to pace themselves well? Such people are often willing to share their ideas with others. Remember, asking for help is a sign of strength!

Eliminating all stress is not only impossible, but it would also come with drawbacks. If you decided to jay-walk across a busy street, a certain degree of stress could help you be more alert to the dangers of oncoming traffic and provide some needed adrenaline to get you moving faster.

Positive Self-Reinforcement and Positive Self-Talk

In the previous chapter, we discussed how rewarding the positive actions of loved ones is more likely to influence constructive, healthy choices and actions. Positive self-reinforcement and healthy self-rewards can also increase the likelihood of desired change in many areas of your own life.

Positive self-talk, generally considered the most powerful self-reinforcement, is also free. Focusing on success breeds success, from the singer who focuses on feeling the music and hitting the notes to the athlete who gets "in the zone." Patting yourself on the back for your efforts and successes, both big and small, helps build confidence, motivation, and determination to continue in your endeavors. Successful people use repeated positive self-talk, like "Way to go!" or "Good job!" or "I will continue to learn from this!"

Reward yourself for your accomplishments, even the "small" victories, like when the kids have been screaming at each other and you kept your cool, or when your spouse or partner lost their temper and you remembered to call a time-out and walk away. Remember when you asserted yourself at work or with your in-laws in a respectful, non-confrontational manner, instead of shoving your feelings down or lashing out.

Depending on your situation, you might treat yourself to a movie, a ballgame, an evening out with friends, or something as simple as a walk on a beautiful day. Would you do it for a good friend? Then why not do it for yourself as well? Try to remember: It's not being selfish to take care of your own needs; it's being self-caring.

When you take care of yourself, you may notice that you get along better with others. Being more consistent in your physical, emotional, mental, and spiritual self-care can help you build a reserve to sustain you in more trying times. Think of this reserve as your own personal savings or investment account, which you make deposits into by regularly taking care of your needs. On some days, you may feel great, with no need to make any withdrawals; but during the inevitable rough patches of life, you will have more energy reserves to draw from. This can help shorten the down periods and enable you to move forward again. Healthy, well-balanced self-care is the key to building resilience for any challenges life may bring.

Positive Self-Reinforcement from the Past

Like Chris Young, singer and co-author of the song "I Hear Voices All the Time," there are numerous people, some living and some no longer here, who have influenced me in my life. I refer to only a small number of them in this book. Often, I find myself remembering a suggestion or word of encouragement from one of them. Sometimes I don't remember who said it, but I do remember the words. You will too.

The more you learn and grow, the more often you will also catch yourself and remember something helpful, regardless of where it came from. Several years ago, I spoke at a national conference for the first time. After the session, a colleague asked me if I had been nervous beforehand. Although I have been nervous or tense on numerous other occasions, this time I was not. I pictured all of those who had influenced me professionally over my long career as if they were standing behind me for support. I had not planned on doing that; it just happened as I was taking the escalator to the meeting hall. Yes, I hear voices—unfortunately, not as often as I would like. And sometimes I hear them, but ignore them out of anger or stubbornness—but I keep learning.

✎ Identify Factors That Contribute to Arguments

Make a list of situations that most frequently invite you to an argument or trigger you to invite someone else to an argument. Leave space between scenarios so you can add more thoughts as you go. Remember, this is not about finding fault; it's about gaining additional insights so you can voice your concerns in a healthy and productive way, and reduce the likelihood of heated arguments. To build upon your progress, you can also refer to comments that you've recorded in your journal from previous chapters.

- What mood are you usually in?

- When are you likely to be hungry, angry (or

annoyed or irritated), lonely, tired, or stressed out severely?

- What comments, words, or actions of others are more likely to invite you to an argument, and by whom?

- What comments, words, or actions of yours are more likely to invite another person to an argument, and who might that person be?

- When in the day are certain arguments more likely to occur and why?

- What days of the week are certain arguments more likely to occur and why?

- During what holiday(s) or other event(s) in the year are certain arguments more likely to occur?

- What other factors can potentially contribute to arguments?

Prepare for Emotionally Charged Situations

Refer to the concerns you listed in the *Why do I argue?* Self-Questionnaire from Chapter One, or the Practice Positive Communication exercise from Chapter Five. Focusing on one scenario at a time, answer the questions below. Be as specific and objective as you can in your answers.

- With whom would you like to be more proactive trying to prevent heated arguments?

- What's the one concern that you want to discuss with them? Begin with the lesser of the potentially charged concerns and build from there.

- What day(s) and time(s) would be best for approaching this person to talk about your concerns?

Next, make a plan for what you're going to say. Record your thoughts as they come to mind. You can come back later to revise, delete, or add other thoughts. You do not have to use every one of the seven guidelines of Positive Communication. Remind yourself that you can always call a time-out if emotions escalate or if you otherwise lose focus. Be brief, and remember to KISS—Keep It Simple, Sweetheart. Long explanations often involve dredging up the past, repeating yourself, or introducing irrelevant concerns and examples, which can make the other person defensive or distracted.

🖊 My plan to be brief is …

Being positive, non-confrontational, and respectful can help you get your concerns really heard and considered. You can also reduce the other person's defensiveness (and potentially your own) by communicating with respect. Use positive statements to communicate what you would like to see happen, rather than what you wouldn't. When you do this, it gives others a better understanding of what you expect from them.

🖊 My plan to be positive, non-confrontational, and respectful is . . .

Others are more likely to really hear and consider your concern when you refer to something specific instead of making a broad statement. Changing a specific behavior can be more tangibly observed and positively reinforced. Try to catch yourself before using absolutes such as "always," "never," "everyone, or "no one." When you express unhappiness with what you think someone else is thinking or feeling, such as, "You think you are so much smarter than everyone else," or "You feel so picked on whenever I try to discuss something," you are entering into a relationship minefield, and also inviting the other person to an argument.

🖊 My plan to refer to a specific concern is …

Label your emotions. Others are likely to acknowledge your emotions more open-mindedly when you present them briefly, calmly, and without judgment or blame. You can find some words to help you label your emotions in Chapter Five.

🖊 My plan to label my emotions is …

Offer an understanding statement. When the other person hears that you understand or are trying to understand what they're saying, it can help them feel less need to defend their own position.

🖊 My plan to offer an understanding statement is …

Accepting partial responsibility for an issue, when appropriate, can often take the wind out of an argument before it gets rolling. This shows that you do not consider yourself perfect, nor are you trying to scapegoat the other person. It can also communicate your willingness to consider how you have contributed to the issue and that you're prepared to cooperate in finding a solution.

Here's an example of taking partial responsibility, modifying an understanding statement, and being positive: "I know, at times, it's hard for me to be open-minded to viewpoints that are different from mine. Help me understand why this is important to you so we can try to find some common ground or points of agreement. Can we agree to take turns with each of us talking about one point at a time, so we can really hear what each other is trying to say?"

✎ My plan for accepting partial responsibility and being positive is . . .

Others are more likely to favorably receive your offers of help when your delivery is calm and straightforward, rather than critical. Questions such as, "Can I help in some way?" or "How can I help?" usually come across as supportive and non-judgmental.

✎ My plan to offer help is . . .

You may find that insights pop into your head at various times of the day (and sometimes at night). Keep a journal or other recording device handy so you can take a few notes and process your thoughts in more detail later. While no situation will repeat itself exactly, you can build upon the experiences you've had. Many researchers emphasize the benefits of role-playing before trying new skills in a potentially stressful situation. Ask a friend to play the role of the individual you would like to improve communication with, and practice using the proactive, positive, and respectful statements you have identified in this exercise. If you are unable to do this, try practicing in front of a mirror. Remember, this is a rehearsal: even the most accomplished musicians, singers, and athletes must practice or rehearse.

When it comes time for the real conversation, briefly explaining that you've written a few thoughts down to help you communicate better can help set the tone for a calmer and more constructive discussion.

After your conversation, take some time to reflect on the positive and respectful communication you used. Then, give yourself some positive self-reinforcement—in writing.

✎ Moving Forward

If there has been a recent argument, it may be helpful to also consider the following:

- What was the first comment made, and by whom? Try to remember the exact words as best as you can.

- What were you attempting to communicate?

- Who made the next comment, as well as any comments after that?

- If a similar situation were to reoccur, what are some proactive steps you could take to keep your reactions in check?

- How might you respond respectfully to increase the likelihood of your concern really being heard?

- If a similar situation were to reoccur, what are some proactive steps you could take to prevent an argument-provoking comment on your part?

Take this one step at a time. You can come back to this activity in a day (or later), and after you have read or reread one or more additional chapters to fine-tune your responses. This can help you continue to build strategies for specific situations in your life.

CHAPTER NINE

Children and Teens

> "Today's youth now love luxury. They have bad manners and contempt for authority. They show disrespect for their elders and love chatter in place of exercise."

Does this sound familiar? Do you know who said it? Socrates did, around 400 BC.

Individuals who criticize young people as a group appear to have forgotten that their own generation was once harshly criticized by the generations that came before them. They also seem to forget the impact of individuals who encouraged and forgave them for their own inexperience. The younger generations are our future, and they need our ongoing investment of time, compassion, and empowerment. The roles of parent and mentor are the most important vocations in the world, regardless of whether or not the person "parenting" has a biological connection to the child; yet no other role seems so puzzling and downright frustrating at times.

The Illusion of Control

After several 2:00 a.m. experiences with my first infant's persistent crying, I had an epiphany about the illusion of being able to control one's child. Yes, I could take her wherever I wanted to, whenever I wanted to, but when she continued to cry in the middle of the night, even after I had changed her diaper, offered her a bottle of warm milk, and sung to her, it seemed I was still powerless to make her comfortable.

As a stay-at-home dad to our first child, I would frequently get up in the middle of weeknights. Sometimes, out of exhaustion or desperation, I would "call for reinforcements," waking my wife for assistance. Her touch could work wonders, but not always. Despite Mom's gentle caress and soothing words, the crying sometimes continued for what seemed an eternity. Four years later, with a second baby (we clearly hadn't learned our lesson), we felt more experienced and confident. And yet, there were still those times in the middle of the night when we were exhausted and frazzled as the crying continued.

The illusion of being able to control our children comes from two sources. The first is from people who are not parents: "If I had kids, I would not let them act like that!" The second is from people who are: "That would not happen to my kid, because I am a very caring parent who tries their best and knows what is going on with their child."

When I would hear or read about a local youth getting arrested, seriously injured, or killed while driving a car or in some other gut-wrenching situation, I might catch myself thinking or saying things like, "Where were the parents?" or, "That could not happen to one of my daughters." Then I would notice the pain in my chest, even when I didn't know any of the people affected by the tragedies, as I felt their pain and feared: *What if that did happen to one of my own children?*

The "illusion of control" over one's children appears to have some valid benefit, albeit temporary, in that it helps us cope with the reality that no one, rich or poor, famous or not, can totally protect their children from all of life's challenges, nor entirely prepare them. Parents can and do provide love, nurture, guidance, support, and many other important things to help their children grow and thrive. Children—and deep down, even teens—want to make their parents proud, and they do learn from what you tell them, but they learn even more from what you do. Keep learning and keep doing

the best you can, and your kids will learn from you as you
continue to grow.

Parents Are the Best Teachers

Parents know their children better than anyone else.
Because of the special emotional bond between parent and
child, parents are uniquely qualified to teach their children
about family values and emotions. They can teach their
children that "to err is human," and that "no one is ever too
old to learn." These phrases have been around for a very
long while, yet parents can be hard on themselves when it
comes to their own perceived errors in parenting or in life.
Remember that mistakes can be blessings in disguise; they
present opportunities for both parent and child.

When my children were aged four and eight, the older
one invited a friend over to play. As I was sitting in our
kitchen, the three children ran past me toward the front door.
I could see that all three would not be able to fit through the
doorway at the same time. I opened my mouth to shout a
warning, but before I could utter a sound, the four-year-old
got bumped face-first into the front of the dishwasher. As she
began to wail in pain, what do you suppose I did? I, the family
counselor, author, and adjunct college instructor jumped up
from my chair and yelled, *"How many times do I have to tell you"*
—wait for it— *"not to run in the house?!"* I know, not the most
original or sympathetic statement. At that point, my youngest
began to cry even louder, and I felt absolutely horrible. I knelt
down to put my arms gently around her. While she continued
to sob loudly, I said in a calmer, more compassionate tone,
"I'm sorry, Daddy's not mad at you." When the crying had
quieted down but not entirely stopped, I repeated, "I am sorry
I yelled at you. I'm not angry at you, but when you hurt, I
hurt."

I have repeated this story many times in parent groups and in individual and family counseling sessions, and I have never had to explain my reaction to another parent. At the moment my then-four-year-old bounced off the dishwasher, all my education, training, and prior experience as a counselor and parent went right out the window. Even now, after all these years, my emotions can still override my judgment and intellect. I can also still be considerably more critical of myself, especially when it comes to interactions with family members, than I would be discussing similar challenges with clients, but I am getting better at this as well.

You don't have to be perfect to be a good parent, friend, sibling, or counselor.

Teachable Moments

Children often respond well to mnemonic devices—those catchy phrases we've been practicing to help us remember things and make learning more enjoyable. As you incorporate mnemonics into your own daily routines, you'll probably start to notice some of them in your conversations with others, especially your children.

For example:

"Matt, can you try to do one thing at a time? You might find your chores go faster once you get started, instead of having to do all of them at the same time."

"Abby, first things first: try to remember, honey, we need to finish our homework first before we start texting friends."

Over time, you will hear your children, teens, and others using some of the same or similar phrases in conversations with you, other family members, and even with their peers. Children and teens *do* hear what you say, even if it doesn't always appear so.

Chores and other obligations can be frustrating, challenging, and sometimes intimidating (even for adults!). Ask your children or teens for their input on how the experience could be made enjoyable, effective, efficient, or just more bearable. This can help them get engaged in the process.

When a child or teen mentions something that happened at school, in the community, or in the news, this can present a favorable time to engage them in conversation. Observing something as you drive, ride on a bus, or watch a television program together can also provide teachable moments. Asking their opinion can help stimulate their thinking and may present an opportunity for you to reinforce some family values and show respect for different points of view. Generally, these teachable moments are more effective if parents keep the conversations brief, unless the child or teen continues it constructively on their end.

Attitude

Some of the many irritations parents have to deal with are the facial expressions, complaints, and whining sounds their children and teens respond with when they're told it's bedtime or that they have to do a certain chore. Expecting the child to do what is asked of them *and* act like they are enjoying it is unintentionally inviting them—and yourself—to an argument.

"You kids think you have it tough. When I was a kid, I walked to school seven miles—uphill both ways." My friend's father actually used that line on his children repeatedly. Some years later when they were older and realized it wasn't possible to go to and from the same place uphill both ways, they confronted him. Ed smiled and replied, "I took a different way home."

As with an adult loved one, a child's attitude is not always about you, or even what you are asking them to do, but may instead be an expression of their struggles, frustrations, fears, or insecurities. Trying as this can be for parents, it may actually be a sign that the child or teen feels safe enough to let their guard down at home instead of maintaining an outwardly cool or indifferent image, as they often do when they are with their peers.[22]

Hormonal changes can also factor into the mood swings of teens and preteens, often confusing them as much as their parents. Remind yourself not to take it personally; this can help you to resist reacting to every sound that comes out of their mouths. Repeating reminders to yourself, like *Don't take it personally,* can be particularly helpful when you're trying to be proactive instead of reactive.

Go Easy on Yourself

Self-care is vital for parents and guardians. It's easy to focus so much on the children that you neglect yourself and your adult relationships. Remember: taking care of yourself is not selfish; it is vital. When parents take care of themselves, they are also modeling the importance of self-care for their children.

I cannot even begin to put into words my admiration for single parents raising their children alone, and for grandparents raising their grandchildren. I have seen many such families and continue to be amazed and inspired by their resilience, resourcefulness, and determination in the face numerous challenges. Not all families possess equal amounts of resources and support. In doing the best they can with what they have, parents and guardians can be powerful, motivating role models for children and teens, which is stronger than any lesson found in a book.

I have read volumes and written many articles about how parents and guardians are affected by a child's chronic illness or disability, which can stretch emotional, financial, and social resources to their limits.[23] Many parents may also be in the sandwich generation, with elderly parents to care for and children to support. Fortunately, there are organizations, self-help programs, and support services that help with a vast spectrum of concerns. You can search for them online or through a local non-profit agency. There are people who *do* understand what you are going through and who can help lessen some of the burdens you carry.

Tantrums and Meltdowns

Strong emotions can be difficult for young children to manage. What some call a temper tantrum—crying, screaming, stomping feet, or rolling around on the floor—is a normal reaction to frustration and anger that begins around the first twelve to eighteen months.

I prefer the term *meltdown*, although at times *tantrum* may be more accurate. According to the American Academy of Pediatrics, these outbursts can become stronger between the ages of two and three years, but taper off once children learn to communicate their needs and wants through words.[24] According to Dr. Jay Hoecker, an emeritus member of the MAYO Clinic's Department of Pediatric and Adolescent Medicine, teaching your baby modified signs from sign language or gestures might help ease frustration by helping them communicate certain needs and wants before they can talk.[25] Information about baby sign language is available online and in books, as well as through other sources, including your child's pediatrician or your primary care doctor.

Some believe that by responding to a meltdown, parents are spoiling or pampering the child, while many others see the response as a teachable moment and opportunity to develop a nurturing child–parent bond. I don't know of any adult who, on occasion, hasn't felt a need to vent and say something like, "These kids are driving me crazy," "I feel like pulling my hair out," or, "I wonder if it's too late to become a nun or priest." Proactive measures can help minimize the likelihood, intensity, and duration of meltdowns for both child and parent.

Daniel Siegel and Tina Payne Bryson, authors of *No-Drama Discipline,* remind us that "discipline" comes from the Latin word *disciplina*, which means teaching, learning, and giving instructions. For many parents, their immediate reaction to a meltdown is to use discipline to get their child to do (or stop doing) something. Rethinking meltdowns as what your child *can't do* at the moment instead of what they *won't* do recognizes that when your child's or teen's emotions are running high, consequences or attempts to teach are ineffective.[26] If your child appears to express anger or frustration, try gently touching or holding them to help them calm down. If you are in a public place, you may need to take them outside, to the car, or to a less public area nearby.

Once they have calmed down, acronyms like HATS— Hungry, Angry, Tired, Scared—can help youngsters identify and communicate emotions they might be struggling with. Offer praise for their ability to identify and share their feelings. Siegel and Bryson also note that once you have been able to connect empathically with your child, their brains become better able to hear and understand as you show them more effective ways to manage their emotions._ If you are going out with your child, be prepared by bringing simple, healthy snacks with you for when your child gets hungry. You can also change location or the subject when necessary. "Look, Hannah, do you see the big bird over there?" Letting your child choose, whenever possible, helps them feel more involved and invested in an activity. For example, instead of asking if they want to take a bath, you might say, "In a few minutes, it will be time for your bath. Would you like to pick which toys to play with?" Bring your child's favorite book or small toy when traveling a significant distance from home, waiting for an appointment, or anywhere the child cannot freely play.

When meltdowns or tantrums seem to occur only in reaction to limits you've set for your child, consider giving them a time-out. Physically take your child away from the problem and give them some time in a pre-designated place to calm down. Briefly state the reason for the time-out and allow them to hold their favorite stuffed toy or other calming object. A general guideline is one minute of time-out for every year of a child's age between ages three and six. For example, a three-year-old would get a three-minute time-out.

Praise your child for being able to calm down after a time-out. This is not about spoiling the child, but rather teaching them how to manage their emotions and behaviors more effectively. Punishing them for a meltdown or using time-outs in reaction to your own parental frustrations may lead them to bottle up feelings, which will lead to bigger meltdowns in the future. If meltdowns persist, speak to your child's primary care doctor or pediatrician to rule out other possible health or behavioral concerns.

Children, teens, and even adults can benefit from a transition time. For example, "Dion, in five minutes, it will be time_to start washing up and getting ready for supper." This can be followed by, "Dion, supper time, come and wash up please." Due to their limited attention spans, younger children will more than likely need a parent or significantly older sibling to escort them to the bathroom, despite their repeated responses of "*I know, I know.*"

The walk and talk—that is, walking with the child as you continue a brief conversation—is likely to be more effective in directing their actions toward the immediate, desired goal.

"Mike, after supper, we will be able to read from one of your favorite books," or, "Emma, after we clean up and eat, we can call Grandma and see when she will be coming to visit us again." A transition time before bed of around fifteen to thirty minutes (with no TV or electronics to over-stimulate the brain) allows more time to shift from other activities, and helps develop patterns that are more conducive to falling asleep. Younger children especially benefit from a pre-bedtime routine of storytelling.

Teach your children that when you say "yes," you mean yes, and when you say "no," you mean no. Avoid making promises you can't keep. Instead, say that you will do your best to go to the movies on Saturday, or whatever it is they are looking forward to.

Praise Effort

The best time to generously praise your child is when you see they are putting in genuine effort, even when they fall short of goals or expectations. I'm not talking about the "I didn't study for the test and got an F" sort of failure. But if they make a genuine effort, they'll often learn more from these types of attempts than from successes. A great mnemonic that can help you remember this concept is FAIL: First Attempt In Learning.

These can be powerful, teachable moments for coping with emotions such as disappointment, frustration, sadness, and even self-loathing. From such opportunities, children can develop frustration-tolerance and determination despite setbacks. These moments can also be learning experiences for parents, and often rewarding ones when the child or teen thanks you in words or with a hug—not for making everything better, but for just being there and listening.

Children and teens need to consistently practice the life skills they are learning. Just as they begin to gain confidence with some skills, they'll often find themselves facing another developmental stage or growth spurt with new challenges and opportunities for learning. With their parents' help and support, they will continue to learn how to label emotions and communicate concerns in ways that can be understood and really heard by others.

For children, playtime provides learning experiences and opportunities to use their imaginations, set goals, and make decisions. Playing with their peers helps them build self-esteem, develop socialization skills, and practice cooperation. According to Jona K. Anderson-McNamee and Sandra J. Bailey of Montana State University:

> "Parent-child play opens doors for the sharing of values, increases communication, allows for teachable moments, and assists in problem solving. Playtime provides opportunities for the parent and child to confront and resolve individual differences, as well as family-related concerns and issues. Finally, it allows the parent to view the world through the eyes of a child again."[27]

Deflect Complaints

Just as the *wax on, wax off* technique from the *Karate Kid* is used to practice deflecting attacks, you can also learn to deflect certain complaints.

Try not to take your family's periodic unhappiness personally. Keep in mind that what may appear as trivial or random complaints to you may be significant issues to a child or teen, and might mask troubling concerns. Again, home is where many children and teens feel unconditionally loved, and therefore safe to let their guard down when they are stressed, troubled, or burdened. As you practice using the communication tools you've been adding to your toolbox, you may find an opportunity to listen with your heart, as well as your ears, to what might be going on with your loved ones.

Examples

Teen's comment: "I hate living in this house with all these rules!"

Prior parent reaction: "I hate going to work some days. Just wait until you get a job and live out in the real world!"

Parent deflecting approach: Remind yourself that you don't have to take this personally, and that all teens feel this way at times. You probably did yourself. Try responding with "I love you. I hear that you are angry. I'm here to listen when you are ready to share your feelings and thoughts with me."

Teen's comment: "Why is everything always my fault?"

Prior parent comment: "Stop feeling so sorry for yourself!"

Parent listening with their heart: "Sue, please tell me what's really troubling you."

✎ Your Turn

- My teen's comment:
- My prior comment:
- My deflecting comment:
- My teen's comment:
- My prior comment:
- My *listening with my heart* comment:

Everyone Needs Healthy Limits

Although children and teens will complain loudly about the unfairness of some consequences, they do recognize on some level that they need and want limits to be set. Limits and family rules serve as a boundary or passageway between safe and unsafe actions, between appropriate and inappropriate social interactions, and between healthy and unhealthy practices.[28]

Siegel and Bryson clarify that the absence of limits creates more stress, and stressed kids tend to be more reactive than proactive in their emotions and interactions with others. When you set limits and boundaries for your children, you teach them the value of predictability and safety in an otherwise chaotic world. As your children learn how to manage their emotions and experience appropriate limits and boundaries, they are also building brain connections that help them to manage challenges more effectively in the future.

Limits can also help teens deal with peer pressure—for example, saying "No thanks" when offered cigarettes, alcohol, or drugs. I have worked with many teens who reported that fear of parental consequences gave them an excuse and effective way to save face whenever they didn't feel confident and secure enough to stand up to peer pressure on their own—they could just blame it on Mom and Dad's "overboard policies!"

As your child or teen matures, there are some issues that you may choose to negotiate with them, such as chores, bedtimes on non-school nights, or how many friends can attend a birthday party. Negotiating, with respectful communication from all parties, shows children and teens that they have input in some of the decisions that affect them. In this way, they learn responsibility and gain self-confidence. Negotiating also can provide teachable moments, as most children and teens are highly motivated to get what they want and often willing to engage in discussions with parents during these times.

Non-negotiable issues may vary from parent to parent, but usually include illegal and unsafe actions. In hindsight, unacceptable and unsafe behaviors can also offer teachable moments, especially if the child or teen genuinely appears to have gained insight from the experience. Natural consequences can include their painful feelings of guilt or embarrassment once they recognize how their behavior, intentional or not, has affected or could have affected themselves or others. It will be up to the parent whether any additional consequences need to be given in these circumstances.

Keep in mind that even if they are genuinely remorseful, teens and young children often know how to influence their parents' feelings to avoid additional consequences. This is part of the limit-testing that some adults may see as manipulative behavior, but which child psychologists also see as a way of children and teens evaluating age-appropriate and safe behaviors.

Teens are not young adults. In the past, child development experts believed young brains physically matured by age eleven or so, and that, basically, youth needed to prepare for independent living by gaining experience, life skills, self-discipline, and emotional maturity. With modern, non-invasive technologies, researchers now have growing evidence that some physical maturation of the brain continues into the late twenties. According to the fact sheet from the US National Institute of Mental Health, *The Teen Brain: Still Under Construction*, the parts of the brain responsible for controlling impulses and planning—the hallmarks of adult behavior—are among the last to mature.[29] This reinforces the idea that teens still need parental guidance and support as they continue to mature mentally and emotionally. This also can help explain why you sometimes feel like pulling your hair out and yelling, *"What were you thinking?!"*

Communicating Without Yelling

Repeating yourself multiple times can actually train a child to wait for a certain number of repeated statements or warnings, and/or a certain decibel level, before they respond. It is an easy pattern for tired and harried parents to fall into, and one that can teach children to wear you down to get what they want.

While parenting styles and philosophies vary from family to family and culture to culture, all children appear to benefit most when their parents are as consistent as possible with family rules and values. Being consistent means adhering to the same principles or course of action without frequently giving in to avoid conflict. You maintain boundaries regularly, not intermittently. Being guilt-tripped by your kids, feeling sorry for them, and overreacting when you are tired or angry are some of the more common reasons parents report for giving in to their child's wants instead of responding to their needs. Occasionally changing your mind or even caving in to a repeated request doesn't necessarily mean you're inconsistent; instead, these occasions provide parents with opportunities to show their children that it is OK to rethink a decision and change one's mind. It can also show them that you make mistakes, try to learn from your mistakes, and that you are, in fact, human.[30]

Changing Your Mind

Although children benefit from consistent parenting, it's not always possible to provide. Situations change—cars break down, someone gets sick, money is tight.

You may have noticed that I use the words "try" and "trying" periodically: "Try to remember to," or "Try to do the best you can." This is not meant solely to encourage and empower you, but also to reflect reality: we do the best we can and, at times, fall short of our goals or expectations. Occasionally, for any number of reasons, you may change your mind, reconsider the information available to you, make a different decision, or choose a different option. We make mistakes more often than we might hope or care to admit. Yes, as a parent or guardian you are the most important person in your child's life, but you are not a Supreme Being.

But children and teens are resilient; they can and will survive your imperfection. Showing that you're an adult work-in-progress actually helps children and teens set healthy, realistic expectations, and recognize that growing up is a lifelong process, not something that just happens and then remains stagnant.

I have attempted, and perhaps not always succeeded, to inject a little humor into this book to lessen some of the tension of dealing with interpersonal conflicts. I have also tried to show that humor, where appropriate, can serve as a healthy coping and teaching tool. According to the University of St. Augustine, laughter releases endorphins (the "feel good" chemicals in the brain that help fight stress and promote a positive mood). Sharing a laugh with a loved one, friend, or coworker can also help you feel more connected to others and form strong and lasting bonds.[31] I believe that in relationships, as well as in parenting and life in general, keeping a sense of humor is also vital to staying sane. Children really seem to enjoy it when parents poke fun at themselves in a healthy way.

When to Seek Help with Kids

There may be times when you have a gut feeling that something else is going on with your child. It may come after you have tried everything you can think of to help them, or you just feel something is wrong. My advice to parents over the years has been to trust their instincts and seek help.

The first step might be consulting your child's pediatrician or primary care physician to see if there is a medical reason for your child's behavior. The doctor may also be able to screen for signs and symptoms of possible depression (which in children and teens may present as agitation instead of fatigue), problems with anxiety, attention deficit hyperactivity disorder (ADHD), learning difficulties, or other issues. In Chapter Ten, we'll explore common parental concerns that may require professional assessment and assistance.

✐ Moving Forward

- One thing my child and I frequently argue about is:
- Next time the issue comes up, I will:
- I will remember to take care of myself by:
- I can picture myself deflecting comments with the visual image of "wax on, wax off," or some other helpful reminders such as:

CHAPTER TEN

What to Do When You Need More Help

This chapter can help you gain insights into frequent conditions that may contribute to your personal and interpersonal stress or conflicts. Note that this chapter presents only a partial list of concerns and symptoms and is not meant to be a substitute for professional assessment.

An additional note of caution: exploring information about relationships or medical or emotional concerns may initially increase your anxiety levels by triggering memories of unpleasant or traumatic experiences, or by fueling tendencies to project worst-case scenarios. Try to remember to take one issue at a time, catch yourself if you see any patterns in your reactions, or use other helpful reminders if you find yourself identifying with any of the following concerns. Also remember to journal throughout this process, especially if you find yourself experiencing strong or painful emotions or memories.

Relationship Issues

Do some arguments seem to trigger comparisons to the past, with thoughts or comments like, "You sound just like my father/mother/ex"? It may be difficult to admit, but all of us bring the past—both the good and the not so good of it—with us into our current relationships. Though you were likely influenced in many positive ways by parents, stepparents, guardians, and others when you were growing up, to some degree each of us also carries negative baggage into our current relationships, whether they be romantic, friendly, or work-related.

Trust issues from past relationships can carry over to your current one and affect how you respond or react to differences of opinion, conflict, perceived criticism, or certain emotions. If some comments seem to result in a strong reaction, perhaps your body or mind is trying to tell you something. It may not be the comment or action itself that you are reacting to, but rather, certain words or actions may have touched a nerve or triggered a memory, whether conscious or hidden.

There are experienced counselors who work with these and other types of issues, and they can help you as an individual, couple, or family to gain valuable insights and build upon the work you have already been doing. If there are relationship concerns between you and a spouse or partner, and that person is not ready to participate with you in counseling at this time, you do not have to wait. You can search for a therapist or counselor who is experienced in working on relationship issues when only one half of a couple is ready to seek help (this is called Unilateral Family Therapy).

Parenting

Continuing to build and practice communication skills between parents, as well as between parents and children, helps to make parenting not only survivable, but also a rewarding and gratifying life experience. However, you may face some challenges that could benefit from additional help. I have never met nor heard of any parents or guardians who have been in complete agreement 100 percent of the time on how to raise a child. Differences of opinion, which may seem relatively small in some areas of life, can take on a great deal more significance and stress when children are involved. When you as a parent or guardian are unable to agree with your partner or find middle ground on issues that are important to both of you, a family counselor or child psychologist can work with you to clarify these areas of concern, set realistic goals, and develop an individualized service plan.

Anxiety Disorders

According to the most recent National Institute of Mental Health-funded National Comorbidity Study (NCS-R Study), 31.2 percent of adults and 32.5 percent of sixteen-year-olds in the United States experience an anxiety disorder at some point in their lives.[32] An anxiety disorder differs from commonplace anxiety (such as being nervous before a first date) in that it lasts a minimum of six months, causes intense fear, and will often get worse without help. The most common anxiety disorders are social anxiety disorder, specific phobias, and panic disorder.

Social Anxiety Disorder

Social anxiety disorder is a noticeable fear or anxiety about one or more social situations where the person is exposed to possible scrutiny by others. Roughly 12 percent of adults and 9.1 percent of teenagers (aged thirteen to eighteen) experience this disorder at some time in their lives.[33] These individuals tend to experience a noticeable fear or anxiety in social interactions, which can include things like having a conversation, meeting with unfamiliar people, being observed while eating or drinking, or performing or speaking in front of others.

People with social anxiety fear that their actions will be humiliating or embarrassing, and that these actions will offend others or lead to rejection, so they either avoid these social situations or endure them with intense discomfort.

In children, the fear or anxiety may be expressed through frequent crying, tantrums, clinginess, shrinking, or failing to speak in social situations.

Specific Phobia

Specific phobia is a noticeable fear or anxiety caused by specific objects or situations, such as flying, heights, animals, injections, or the sight of blood. In children, the fear or anxiety may be expressed by crying, tantrums, freezing, or clinging. 12.5 percent of adults and 19.3 percent of teenagers (aged thirteen to eighteen) experience a specific phobia at some time in their lives.[34]

With a specific phobia, the phobic object or situation almost always provokes immediate fear or anxiety. The person avoids the object or situation, or endures it with intense pain. Their reaction is persistent and causes clinically significant distress or impairment in social, occupational, or other important areas of functioning. Other examples of specific phobias can include the fear of insects, storms, elevators, or enclosed spaces. For children, they might include the fear of loud sounds and costumed characters such as clowns.

Panic Disorder

A person with a panic disorder experiences recurring panic or anxiety attacks. They produce a sudden surge of intense fear or discomfort. This may include chest pain, a pounding heart, shortness of breath, abdominal distress, sweating, and a fear of losing control. An estimated 4.7 percent of adults and 2.3 percent of adolescents experience a panic disorder at some time in their lives.[35]

Posttraumatic Stress Disorder (PTSD)

PTSD can develop after a person has experienced or witnessed a traumatic event. It can also develop after learning that a traumatic event occurred to a close family member or friend. Symptoms may include recurring distressful flashbacks, memories, or dreams of the event, as well as persistent feelings of fear, horror, anger, guilt, or shame. 6.8 percent of adults and 5 percent of teenagers (aged thirteen to eighteen) develop PTSD at some point in their lives.[36]

Major Depressive Disorder

Major depressive disorder (often referred to as "depression") differs from the occasional sadness or down feelings everyone feels in that it persists and interferes with everyday life, including work, school, sleeping, eating, and/or the enjoyment of once pleasurable activities. Approximately 7.1 percent of adults and 3.2 percent of teenagers in the United States experience a major depressive episode at some time in their lives, with women 70 percent more likely than men to experience depression.[37]

Getting Help

Your primary care physician or pediatrician can help determine if any or most of the preceding symptoms are the result of an underlying medical problem or indications of a disorder, trauma, or clinical depression. They can also discuss helpful treatment options with you.

If you are concerned that a loved one or friend may be currently thinking of harming themselves or committing suicide, call 911 or another emergency service. Do not try to decide if you think they may or may not actually act on these feelings. Your phone call will bring the help of professionals who are trained to assess these situations.

I know many people who have taken such action on behalf of a friend or loved one, and they consistently report that the professionals assured them they had done the right thing by calling for help. This is regardless of whether the individual was later assessed as needing inpatient hospitalization, or assessed and discharged with outpatient resources put in place for ongoing help.

Alcohol and Drug Use Disorders

Alcohol and other drug-use disorders affect people of all income and education levels, as well as all cultural and racial backgrounds. Of all the people with a substance use disorder in the United States, 61.7 percent (12.2 million) had an alcohol-use disorder only, and 26.4 percent (5.2 million) had a drug-use disorder only. In other words, there were more than twice as many people with alcohol-use disorders than with all other drug-use disorders combined.[38]

Has your or a loved one's alcohol or drug use caused or contributed to:

- Repeated absences from work or school, a decline in work or school performance, or the neglect of household or parenting duties?
- Ongoing social or family problems?
- Physical or psychological problems?

Have you or a loved one:

- Repeatedly drank or used drugs in physically dangerous situations, such as driving or on certain jobs?

- Repeatedly tried and failed to cut down or control your use, or used larger amounts or over a longer period of time than you intended? These are signs of losing control.

- Continued using despite it causing or contributing to problems?

- Used more to get the same effect, or found that the same amount results in a decreased effect? This is a sign your body has developed a tolerance.

- Experienced withdrawal symptoms when you tried to stop or cut down? This indicates a physical dependence and may require medically supervised detoxification to prevent a withdrawal that is very uncomfortable (from opioids) or potentially life-threatening (from alcohol, tranquilizers in the benzodiazepine class, or barbiturates).

In my experience, one of the most common factors contributing to ongoing marital or familial conflicts is alcohol and/or substance abuse, because this problem affects all facets of society. I would like to tell you that if you are concerned about someone else's drinking or drug use—whether it be a teen or adult child, spouse, partner, parent, sibling, or friend—you are probably jumping to conclusions and overreacting. However, having worked with over two thousand family members concerned about someone else's drinking or drug use, I am hard-pressed to think of anyone who did not have significant reasons for their concerns.

Trust your gut and ask for help. Remember, it's a sign of strength.

Co-occurring Disorders

I think there should be a law that gives anyone experiencing a distressing problem a break from all other major issues for at least one year. Unfortunately, life doesn't work that way. One or more disorders may be present at the same time with some similar or overlapping symptoms. My training has shown me that good treatment begins with good assessment.

When I meet with a new client, I frequently give this example to demonstrate the need for a professional, comprehensive assessment regardless of the presenting concern that brings them to their first counseling session. I say something like:

> "Let's say you felt ill and went to your primary care clinician. They take your temperature and note you have a fever. Next, your throat is checked and found to be red and inflamed. Should the examination end at that point? What if there is an additional reason for an elevated temperature? So, they ask a few more questions, look in each ear, then examine your abdomen. When the right side of your abdomen is pressed, you let out a loud yelp. This might suggest the need for further tests to rule out appendicitis. Had the examination or assessment ended when the first condition appeared to explain your concerns, another condition could have, for the time being, been missed."

Physical Violence

Relationship violence can happen to anyone of any age, education level, financial status, race, or culture. The Centers for Disease Control and Prevention, which reports on intimate partner violence, cites that one out of three women and one in ten men in the United States will experience intimate partner violence in their lifetime.[39] Granted, men are less likely than women to report being assaulted by a spouse or partner. They may be embarrassed to admit to being abused, or fear they'll be accused of being the abuser.

Domestic violence also includes slapping, grabbing, pushing, twisting arms or fingers, and/or issuing threats. All the professionals I know agree that physical violence is not acceptable, no matter what unfortunate experiences the perpetrator may have had or what other good qualities they may possess. Often the perpetrator will also seek to control the victim by restricting access to finances (cash, checkbooks, credit and debit cards), and attempting to isolate the victim from friends and relatives.

When violence or the threat of violence occurs, it can be vital not to go to arguments you are invited to, and instead use great caution in expressing your feelings or opinions. Seek help! You can reach domestic violence service agencies by phone, in person, or online. You may feel safer using a computer at your local library or borrowing a friend's smart device to eliminate the possibility of being monitored. Another option is to ask a trusted friend or relative to seek out information about local domestic violence services for you.

One of the first priorities that domestic violence specialists emphasize is to develop a safety plan. There are experienced people who can help you develop an individualized and detailed safety plan which would include the following:[40]

1. A list of two or more places you can go to if you need to leave your home immediately.

2. Phone numbers of friends, family members, and/or a local domestic violence hotline you can call *after* you leave your home.

Remember that calling 911 will bring help from the police, who can put you in contact with additional resources. Do this if at any time you feel your safety or your children's safety is threatened and you are unable to leave your home.

Is there a neighbor you can confide in, and who can call 911 for you if they hear angry or violent noises? If you have children, can you teach them to call 911 if you are unable to, giving them a codeword or phrase that you will use if you need help?

If the perpetrator has convinced you that you don't deserve help or that no one will believe you, then get help for your children's sake. Children with a stable protective parent are more likely to be resilient, despite being exposed to intimate partner violence. This includes greater feelings of self-worth, increased self-confidence, and a commitment to breaking the cycle of violence. Above all, try to remember that no matter what anyone might say, it is not your fault and you do not have to deal with this alone.

We All Need Help Sometimes

Self-help books can provide a great deal of information, guidance, and support; they have for me. Yet sometimes, you may feel you need something else, either for yourself or someone you care about. No matter how much you try not to go to every argument you are invited to, there can be times when some professional help may be needed to supplement the additional skills you have been acquiring and using to the best of your abilities.

You shouldn't be expected to identify or assess every single one of your own emotional concerns, or those of your loved ones, any more than you would be expected to self-diagnose every health concern, such as diabetes or high blood pressure. This applies to professionals as well. I had assessed countless cases of ADHD in others long before I was able to acknowledge and accept it in myself.

No physician has the expertise, experience, and impartiality to treat all their own health concerns or those of their family members. From time to time, each of us needs and deserves some form of assistance.

As A.A. Milne has reminded us:

"Pooh, what's the bravest thing you've ever said?" asked Piglet.

"Help," said Pooh.

Remember, asking for help is a sign of strength.

How to Find Help

When trying to find help for themselves or a loved one, many people impulsively do a quick internet search and begin calling agencies, only to find themselves overwhelmed and confused. The following can help you navigate through the many types of services in your area.

Contact Your Health Insurance Company

A more direct approach may be to contact your health insurance company. Look on your insurance card for the phone number of Mental Health (or Behavioral Health) and Substance Abuse services or MH/SA (or BH/SA) services. Be specific when you call. I recommend writing down your questions and thoughts beforehand.

Explain that you want the names and phone numbers of counseling agencies or individual counselors experienced in assessing and treating specific issues such as depression, anxiety, substance abuse, and/or counseling (specify for child, teen, couples, or family). If you are not specific about requesting a counselor experienced in these areas, you may be referred to an agency or individual who may or may not be sufficiently qualified or experienced to treat your main concerns. Your insurance company's database will usually have more detailed and up-to-date information on counselors' and psychologists' areas of specialty than your paper directory.

Nevertheless, I have spoken with hundreds of people who followed these steps and attempted to contact several therapists and/or agencies, only to be told they were no longer providers for that particular insurance plan or did not provide that particular service. If this occurs, take a deep breath or even a short break, and try to remember you are still making progress by narrowing down your search. Many behavioral health agencies provide services for individuals and families who don't have insurance. They can often assist you in obtaining medical insurance in your state (if you're located in the US).

Ask for Referrals

You may also wish to ask your primary care doctor, pediatrician, clergy member, or other trusted professional if they know of a local agency or a particular counselor whom they know from experience and would feel comfortable referring you to. One of the best ways to find a therapist is to ask someone you know with similar concerns for the name of someone they found helpful (or not helpful, so you can avoid them). You may encounter a waiting list for one or more of the places or persons you are contacting. It is quite appropriate to get your name or loved one's name on a waiting list of more than one agency or counselor in private practice. Then, with all things being equal, take the first available appointment and cancel your other appointments.

When seeking help, be prepared to advocate for your needs (or those of your child). If you do not think your questions or opinions are being heard, clearly state that to the professional, using positive and respectful language. The client-counselor and patient-physician relationships become considerably more productive when clients and family members believe they are being heard and understood, and when they understand what the professional is recommending.

Like many of my colleagues, I was trained early in my career to focus on how parents contributed to the illness or conditions of their child. Not surprisingly, I often found myself frustrated when dealing with parents. What I didn't understand was that in those interactions, I was primarily focused on telling them of what I, "the professional," thought they needed to learn and do to help their child. When parents didn't act how I thought they should, or as quickly as I thought they should, it reinforced my misperceptions that they were being resistant, adding further to my frustration. I didn't consider how the youth's illness or other conditions also affected the parents, and I suspect my misguided approach unintentionally added to their distress.

Since reviewing the literature on how a child's chronic illness or other serious condition affects their parents and listening to over one thousand parents of teenagers in inpatient and outpatient settings, my focus has humbly changed. I now ask myself, "How does the illness or condition affect the child and their family members, and what can I do to help and support each of them?"[41] I have learned that when people express concerns to me about their loved ones, they are seldom overreacting. When they tell me that something else is wrong with their loved one or friend, my response is now,

"You have my attention. Together we can shed more light on what you are dealing with and explore options together."[42]

Patients and clients of counselors are entitled to get a second opinion on any assessment or treatment options. I don't recommend you rush to seek out another professional if your situation isn't improving as fast as you want it to. (I can almost guarantee change will not happen fast enough.) However, you may want to consider seeking another opinion if you continue to feel that your current professional is not hearing you or taking you seriously, or if you continue to disagree with their assessment or recommendations.

Many people have found self-help groups such as Alcoholics Anonymous (www.aa.org) and Narcotics Anonymous (www.na.org) very helpful for dealing with their own alcohol or other drug problem, and Al-Anon (www.al-anon.org) and Nar-Anon (www.nar-anon.org) very understanding and supportive in dealing with the effects of a loved one's drinking or drug problem. Alateen, a part of Al-Anon, is for teenagers who have been affected by someone else's drinking or drug use.

Self-help and support groups, while varied in their approaches, generally focus on people sharing their constructive experiences of coping with challenges and significantly improving the quality of their lives. Many organizations also offer online group support meetings for convenience, or for those who are unsure if they want to attend or are not yet ready. I have also helped many of my clients find online support from national associations that deal with anxiety, major depression, post-traumatic stress disorder, and chronic medical conditions, including some uncommon and rare diseases.

A note of caution with online searches: there can also be a great deal of well-meaning information that is misleading or inaccurate. That is why I have referred to national associations and established self-help programs. You can find a list of trusted and reliable resources on my website, www.jerrymanney.com/resources.

As mentioned in Chapter Four, Robert J. Meyers, author of *Get Your Loved One Sober*, collaborated with other scientists and clinicians to develop the Community Reinforcement And Family Training (CRAFT) therapeutic model, which uses "scientifically validated behavioral principles to reduce the loved one's substance use and to encourage him or her to seek treatment."[43] Studies suggest the CRAFT program is successful 64 to 74 percent of the time in engaging loved ones in treatment, which is significantly higher than other approaches. All the concerned significant others who participated in the CRAFT program in those studies reported significant reductions in their own anger, anxiety, depression, and negative physical symptoms, regardless of whether their loved ones entered treatment or not.

Sexual Harassment

Sexual harassment is a form of sex discrimination and violates Title VII of the Civil Rights Act when it occurs in the workplace.[44] The US Equal Employment Opportunity Commission, EEOC, defines sexual harassment as unwelcome sexual advances, requests for sexual favors, and other verbal or physical conduct of a sexual nature when any of the following apply:

1. Submission to such conduct is a term or condition of an individual's employment. The requirement may be explicit, implicit, or implied.

2. Conduct of a sexual nature has the purpose or effect of unreasonably interfering with a person's work performance.

3. Conduct of a sexual nature creates an intimidating, hostile, or offensive working environment.

Unwelcome means unwanted sexual conduct or inappropriate sexual talk. If you consider the behavior unwanted—it is unwanted! Sexual harassment can happen to anyone, whether you are a woman or a man, and whether the harasser is of the same or opposite sex as you. Sexual harassment can include direct or indirect threats or bribes for sexual activity. It can also include sexually suggestive jokes, innuendos, comments, as well as unwelcome touching or brushing up against you. If you have been subjected to unwanted sexual, physical, or verbal behavior at your job, you have the right to get help through your manager. If your manager is the person who is harassing you, you can get help through your Human Resources Department or the Equal Employment Opportunity Commission (EEOC), or through your state's fair employment practices agency.

Employee Assistance Programs

Employee assistance programs (EAPs) are valuable, confidential resources for various life and family issues. Over the past sixty-five years, EAPs have been adopted by over 85 percent of employers of five hundred or more employees.[45] These organizations recognize that helping employees increases productivity, reduces absenteeism, increases satisfaction with work and life issues, and improves team relationships. Many employers offer several free in-person or phone-counseling sessions through their EAP.[46]

Don't Wait to Seek Help

Regardless of which type of approach you or your loved one initially decide on, at that time it becomes the best choice. First of all, you and/or your loved one will be getting much-needed help and support! Second, collaborating with professionals and getting to know others with similar concerns can provide opportunities for exploring additional options.

✐ Moving Forward

- Reflect on any signs you've observed that may indicate you or a loved one need additional help.

- If you do believe you or they need more help, take a moment right now to brainstorm 2–3 resources you can consult and research further. Your list can include websites, organizations, or trusted individuals whom you can ask for help.

- Briefly reflect on a time when you needed help and asked for it. How did it feel? What was the outcome? Can you do it again for your current challenges?

CHAPTER ELEVEN

Keep Things in Perspective

When someone says to me, "Things were different in the old days; people trusted each other. We didn't have to lock our doors at night," I reply, "Maybe that was your experience. As a therapist, however, I can tell you there are many people of earlier and recent generations who have shared their stories of physical and sexual abuse." These are not new problems. Yet for numerous reasons, these and other violent crimes, such as domestic assault, are often not reported or are reported but not believed. Worse, especially in cases where women are the victims of rape or domestic violence, the victims are often blamed for enticing or provoking their attackers. It is truly a profound and privileged experience when an individual trusts you enough to tell you their story. Over time, many brave individuals have come forward to help break stereotypes, dispel myths, and foster much-needed societal change.

Depending on your perspective of the world today, it may be the best of times or the worst of times. The way you view the world around you can influence how you cope with the challenges and opportunities life presents and how you approach your interactions with others.

You only have to listen to the evening news or read the daily headlines to be bombarded with a litany of tragic accidents, murders, armed conflicts, and other depressing events. How do you not let the day-to-day stresses and problems of home, job, country, and the world get to you and negatively impact your interactions with others? We also live in an electronic age that has helped speed advances in medicine, communication, automobile safety, and countless other areas. Social media has enabled people to stay in contact with numerous long-distance friends and family members. Digital video can be uploaded and shared with others throughout the world within seconds. These developments are nothing short of amazing!

So, are things better or worse now than they were in the "olden days"? It all depends on your perspective. More importantly, how you view the world around you can also influence, to varying degrees, how you approach your interactions with others and how you cope with the challenges and opportunities life presents.

Face Everything and Reconcile

Fear can contribute to communication problems by triggering angry reactions or hindering open and assertive expression. We can become fearful when we're unsure how a loved one, friend, coworker, or employer will respond to our concerns. As we continue to learn and practice the tools we are acquiring, we can transform our fear into Face Everything (one step at a time) and Reconcile.

Social Norms Theory

Social norms theory, developed by Perkins and Berkowitz, is based upon the premise that much of a younger person's behavior is influenced by their perception of what is normal or typical. If they think a certain behavior is typical of their peers, they may be more likely to engage in that type of behavior.[47]

One example is this: many teens think most of the students at their own school abuse alcohol and use marijuana. Youth often overestimate the number of their fellow students who are engaging in high-risk activities. This can increase feelings of peer pressure to engage in some of these behaviors.

Since 1975, the University of Michigan has conducted

yearly surveys (Monitoring the Future Study) of a cross-section of eighth- to twelfth-graders concerning substance abuse in the United States. Many researchers use data from this survey in their work. In the 2018 Monitoring the Future Study, 89.5 percent of eighth-graders, 72.5 percent of tenth-graders, and 64.1 percent of twelfth-graders had not used marijuana in the past year, and appear to be in the distinct majority of youth who continue to make healthy daily decisions about not using marijuana.[48] Additionally:

- 93.5 percent of eighth-graders, 79.1 percent of tenth-graders, and 66.1 percent of twelfth-graders surveyed had never been drunk;

- 90.1 percent of eighth-graders, 82.0 percent of tenth-graders, and 76.2 percent of twelfth-graders surveyed had never smoked cigarettes;

- 73.1 percent of twelfth-graders said that they preferred to date people who did not smoke.[49]

In one graduate-level college course I co-taught solely for teachers, nearly all the teachers appeared discouraged and were highly vocal in their belief that most students abused alcohol and used marijuana until I showed them the data from this survey. It opened their eyes and minds to how misperceptions could affect even dedicated professionals. How does your perspective of the younger generation influence your attitudes and actions?

Practicing Gratitude Can Improve Relationships

Making the time to record and review a list of things you are grateful for can have numerous benefits. Research increasingly shows that practicing gratitude can have dramatic and lasting positive effects in a person's life, making them happier and more pleasant to be around.[50] Gratitude can also lower blood pressure, improve immune functioning, promote happiness and well-being, and spur acts of helpfulness, generosity, and cooperation. Additionally, gratitude reduces your lifetime risk for depression, anxiety, and substance-abuse disorders.[51] Like the pickle jar analogy, an attitude of gratitude also can help fill the temporary void when you are trying so hard to let go of anger, fear, discouragement, or other trying emotions, all of which can help you keep your life and relationships in a more meaningful perspective.

✐ Can you take a few moments to begin a list of what you are grateful for? Rather than stating general areas such as, "I am grateful (or thankful) for my health, family, friends, etc.," try to use specific examples. If you only have a minute or so now to record in your journal, or make a mental list, give it a try—you can continue whenever you want.

- Today, I am grateful for:
- I realize that:

Keeping Perspective as You Move Forward

When you choose not to go to every argument you're invited to, when you decide not to invite others to arguments, and when you try to truly accept that you can influence but not control what someone else thinks or does, you are in effect acknowledging that you are not an all-powerful being.

Giving up the illusion that you can control someone else's actions will take a tremendous load from your shoulders. When you acknowledge that you do not have all the answers in life, you no longer bear the burden of trying to be a superhero who has no superpowers. But if you acknowledge that you are not a god or some all-powerful entity that can "will" change to happen in a loved one, where does that leave you?

Without some degree of faith and hope for positive change, you can easily revert back to old patterns of trying to coerce others to change, or wind up feeling hopeless. "I give up. She will never change!" You may be right. You may not be. My experience in many years as a counselor has shown me that change is always possible. While I have heard many utter, "They will never change," experience has shown that this statement was usually made out of frustration as the individual attempted again to find ways to *make* the other person change, which inevitably resulted in more arguments, hurt feelings, and discouragement. People can change when they're ready to change, and when they are exposed to the conditions and support conducive for change to occur.

If you continue to develop and nurture a belief, faith, philosophy, or grander view of life that can support you through hard times, you can also picture your loved ones having a similar opportunity for such support when they are ready. Knowing that God or some other guiding force is also available to those you care about can make a decisive difference when you feel the tug of old, unsatisfactory patterns pulling you backward. Consider support systems of family and friends, personal beliefs, and gratitude lists like a type of savings account that can add to the quality of your life. They are supports you can draw upon when you are feeling down, tired, stressed, or discouraged.

A colleague of mine once mentioned to me that she'd had a terrible dream. I didn't think much of her statement, as this happens to all of us from time to time. She followed up by saying: "I dreamt I was God." Now that got my attention. I thought, "How was dreaming of being God such a terrible experience?" She said:

> "I dreamt I was in heaven and people
> down on earth were praying because there

had been a bad drought, and if it didn't rain soon, their crops would wither and die. Other people were praying because it had been raining so much for so long their houses were on the verge of being swept away. Still others were praying because it was so cold that they didn't know if they would have enough fuel to keep from freezing to death, while others prayed because it had been so hot their crops were rotting in the fields. And the dream went on and on. When I finally awoke, I was exhausted, but when I realized I was dreaming, I was so happy I wasn't God because I am not qualified."

Although you can continue learning constructive ways to truly influence, support, and assist others, you are not qualified to make another human change, or to live someone else's life for them. Fortunately, you can continue to focus on changing yourself and leave the job of changing others to someone (or something) eminently more qualified.

We end the last chapter of this book as you begin the next chapter of your life. Like a pebble tossed into a pond, every positive action you take in changing your communication with others also has a ripple effect. How you interact with others creates a dynamic that continues to grow from the source, just like the concentric circles around the pebble. It changes the dynamics of future interactions where communication will no longer be the same as it was in the past. You can set in motion a change in your own communication style that has the distinct potential to influence positive change in those around you.

Remember, Positive Communication *is* contagious. You *can* contribute to a healthy epidemic. *This* is the time.

FURTHER READING

Aalto University, *Movie Research Results: Multitasking Overloads the Brain—The Brain Works Most Efficiently When It Can Focus on a Single Task for a Longer Period of Time*, ScienceDaily, 25 April 2017.

American Academy of Pediatrics, "Temper Tantrums: A Normal Part of Growing Up," AAP Publications, Elk Grove Village, IL.

Anderson-McNamee, Jona, K., Bailey, Sandra J., *The Importance of Play in Early Childhood Development*, Montana State University Extension, April 2010.

Berkowitz, Alan, D., "An Overview of the Social Norms Approach," in Lederman, Linda, C., Stewart, Lea P., Goodhart, F., and Lartman, L., *Changing the Culture of College Drinking: A Socially Situated Prevention Campaign*, Chapter 13, Hampton Press, Cresskill, NJ, p 196.

Center for Behavioral Health Statistics and Quality, 2017 National Survey on Drug Use & Health, Maryland, 2018.

Centers for Disease Control and Prevention, The National Intimate Partner and Sexual Violence Survey (NISVS), 2011, Summary Reports, 2014, https://www.cdc.gov/violenceprevention/datasources/nisvs/

Consumer Healthcare Products Association, Stop Medicine Abuse, www.stopmedicineabuse.org

Billikopf, Gregorio, *Party-Directed Mediation, Facilitating Dialogue Between Individuals*, University of California, Modesto, Division of Agriculture and Natural Resources, 3rd ed., 2014.

DeSantis, Richard P., Manney, Gerald J., "Parental Distress: Moving from Reaction to Response," Adolescence Magazine, July 1993.

Emmons, Robert, Stern, Robin, "Gratitude as a Psychotherapeutic Intervention," Journal of Clinical Psychology, Vol 69 (8) August 2013.

Fisher, Roger, Ury, William, Patton, Bruce, *Getting to Yes: Negotiating Agreement Without Giving In*, 3rd ed., Penguin Books, New York, 2011.

Harvard Health Publishing, Harvard Medical School, "Understanding the Stress Response," March 1, 2011, https://www.health.harvard.edu/staying-healthy/understanding-the-stress-response

Hayes, J., "Foreword," in Workplace Conflict and How Businesses Can Harness It To Thrive, CPP, Global Human Capital Report, July 2008.

Hoecker, Jay L., MD, "Is Baby Sign Language Worthwhile?" Mayo Clinic, http://www.mayoclinic.org, 2014.

Kushner, Harold, S., *When Bad Things Happen to Good People*, Avon Books, New York, 1981.

Manney, Gerald J., "Partnering with Parents," EAP Digest, Spring 2010.

Meyers, Robert J., Wolfe, Brenda L., *Get Your Loved One Sober: Alternatives to Nagging, Pleading and Threatening*, Hazelden, Center City MN, 2004.

Meyers, Robert J., and Smith, Jane Ellen, Motivating Substance Abusers to Enter Treatment: Working with Family Members [geared toward professionals], The Guilford Press, New York, 2008, pp 111–115.

"Monitoring the Future: A Continuing Study of American Youth," University of Michigan, www.monitoringthefuture.org tables and figures, data tables, 2018.

National Institute of Mental Health, The National Comorbidity Study (NCS-R), https://www.nimh.nih.gov/

National Institute of Mental Health, "The Teen Brain: Still Under Construction," Publication NO. 11-4929, 2011, https://www.nimh.nih.gov/

Sampl, Susan, Kadden, Ronald, *Motivational Enhancement Therapy and Cognitive Behavioral Therapy for Adolescent Cannabis Users: 5 Sessions (MET/CBT 5)*, School of Medicine, Substance Abuse and Mental Health Administration (SAMHSA), Center for Substance Abuse Treatment (CSAT).

Siegel, Daniel J, MD, Payne Bryson, Tina, PhD, *No-Drama Discipline*, Bantam Books, 2014.

Stalder, Daniel, R., "The Bias of Thinking You Can Decode Body Language," Psychology Today Blog, July 25, 2018.

US Bureau of Labor Statistics, Employer Provided Quality-of-Life Benefits, March 2016.

US Equal Employment Opportunity Commission, Title VII of the Civil Rights Act 1964, https://www.eeoc.gov/statutes/title-vii-civil-rights-act-1964

Verma, Ragini, Gur, Ruben, C., Gur, Raquel E., et al, Brain Connectivity Study Reveals Striking Differences Between Men and Women, Pearlman School Medicine News Release, University of Pennsylvania, December 2, 2013.

Watts, Richard E., *Being a Therapeutic Chameleon: An Encouragement-Focused Perspective*, Sam Houston State University, Presentation November 22, 2014, https://alfredadler.edu/dr-richard-watts-presentations

ENDNOTES

1 Robert J. Meyers and Brenda L. Wolfe, *Get Your Loved One Sober, Alternatives to Nagging, Pleading and Threatening*, (Center City, MN: Hazelden 2004), p 16.

2 Aalto University, *Movie Research Results: Multitasking Overloads the Brain—The Brain Works Most Efficiently When It Can Focus on a Single Task for a Longer Period of Time*, ScienceDaily (April 25, 2017).

3 Gregorio Billikopf, *Party-Directed Mediation, Facilitating Dialogue between Individuals*, 3rd ed., p 67. University of California, Modesto, Division of Agriculture and Natural Resources, 2014.

4 Susan Sampl and Ronald Kadden, *Motivational Enhancement Therapy and Cognitive Behavioral Therapy for Adolescent Cannabis Users: 5 Sessions (MET/CBT 5)*, School of Medicine, Substance Abuse and Mental Health Administration (SAMHSA), Center for Substance Abuse Treatment (CSAT).

5 "Understanding the Stress Response," Harvard Health Publishing (March 1, 2011).

6 Richard E. Watts, Being a Therapeutic Chameleon: An Encouragement-Focused Perspective, Sam Houston State University, Presentation 11.22.14, p 32, https://alfredadler.edu/dr-richard-watts-presentations.

7 Richard P. DeSantis and Gerald J. Manney, *Suspended Adolescence: Understanding and Dealing with Teenage Substance Abusers* (Dublin, NH: Turn on screen reader support, 2007), p 54.

8 Ibid, p 51.

9   Daniel R. Stalder, "The Bias of Thinking You Can Decode Body Language," Psychology Today Blog (July 25, 2018).

10 Ragini Verma, PhD, Ruben, C. Gur, PhD, Raquel E. Gur, MD, et al, "Brain Connectivity Study Reveals Striking Differences Between Men and Women," Pearlman School Medicine News Release, University of Pennsylvania (December, 2, 2013).

11 Jeff Hayes, "Foreword" in *Workplace Conflict and How Businesses Can Harness It To Thrive*, CPP, Global Human Capital Report (2008).

12 Meyers and Wolfe, *Get Your Loved One Sober*, pp xvii–xix.

13 Robert J. Meyers and Jane Ellen Smith, *Motivating Substance Abusers to Enter Treatment, Working with Family Members* (New York: The Guilford Press, 2008), pp. 111–115.

14 Billikopf, Party-Directed Mediation, p 95.

15 Roger Fisher, William Ury, and Bruce Patton Bruce, *Getting to Yes: Negotiating Agreement Without Giving In*, 3rd ed., (New York: Penguin Books, 2011), p. 855.

16 Ibid, p 767.

17 Ibid, p 68.

18 Bianca P. Acevedo, Michael J. Poulin, Nancy L. Collins, and Lucy L. Brown, "After the Honeymoon: Neural and Genetic Correlates of Romantic Love in Newlywed Marriages." Frontiers in Psychology 11 (2020); p. 634.

19 Lauren J.N. Brent, Steve W.C. Chang, Jean-François Gariépy, and Michael L. Platt, "The Neuroethology of Friendship." Annals of the New York Academy of Sciences 1316, no. 1 (2013): pp.1–17. https://doi.org/10.1111/nyas.12315.

20 Julianne Holt-Lunstad, Timothy Smith, and J. Bradley Layton, "Social relationships and mortality risk: a meta-analytic review." SciVee, 2010. https://doi.org/10.4016/19911.01.

21 Harold S. Kushner, *When Bad Things Happen to Good People*, (New York: Avon Books 1981), p 84.

22 DeSantis and Manney, *Suspended Adolescence*, p 51.

23 Richard P. DeSantis and Gerald J. Manney, "Parental Distress: Moving from Reaction to Response," Adolescence Magazine, July 1993, pp 29–52.

24 American Academy of Pediatrics, "Temper Tantrums: A Normal Part of Growing Up."(Elk Grove Village, IL: AAP Publications 1989).

25 Jay L. Hoecker, "Is Baby Sign Language Worthwhile?" Mayo Clinic, 2014. https://www.mayoclinic.org/healthy-lifestyle/infant-and-toddler-health/expert-answers/baby-sign-language/faq-20057980.

26 Daniel J. Siegel, MD, Tina Payne Bryson, PhD, *No-Drama Discipline*, Bantam Books, 2014.

27 Jona K. Anderson-McNamee and Sandra J. Bailey, *The Importance of Play in Early Childhood Development*, Montana State University Extension, April 2010.

28 DeSantis and Manney, Suspended Adolescence, p 47.

29   National Institute of Mental Health, "The Teen Brain: Still Under Construction." Publication No. 11-4929, 2011.

30   DeSantis and Manney, *Suspended Adolescence*, p 48.

31   "10+ scientifically proven ways laughter can relieve stress." University of St. Augustine for Health Sciences. (2020, August 12). Retrieved December 11, 2021, from https://www.usa.edu/blog/how-laughter-can-relieve-stress/.

32   National Institute of Mental Health, *The National Comorbidity Study* (NCS-R).

33   Ibid.

34   Ibid.

35   Ibid.

36   Ibid.

37   Ibid.

38   Center for Behavioral Health Statistics and Quality, *2017 National Survey on Drug Use & Health*, 2018.

39   Sharon G. Smith, Xinjian Zhang, Kathleen C. Basile, Melissa T. Merrick, Jing Wang, Marcie-jo Kresnow, Jieru Chen, National Intimate Partner and Sexual Violence Survey: 2015 Data Brief.

40   "Create a Safety Plan." The Hotline, November 29, 2021. https://www.thehotline.org/plan-for-safety/create-a-safety-plan/.

41 Gerald J. Manney, "Partnering with Parents," EAP Digest, Spring 2010.

42 Ibid.

43 Meyers and Wolfe, *Get Your Loved One Sober*, p xvii.

44 US Equal Employment Opportunity Commission, *Title VII of the Civil Rights Act 1964*, https://www.eeoc.gov/statutes/title-vii-civil-rights-act-1964.

45 US Bureau of Labor Statistics, *Employer Provided Quality-of-Life Benefits*, March 2016.

46 Workplace Outcome Suite (WOS), a five-item measure tool, Federal Occupational Health.

47 Alan D. Berkowitz, "An Overview of the Social Norms Approach," in *Changing the Culture of College Drinking: A Socially Situated Prevention Campaign* by Lederman and Stewart, Chapter 13. (Cresskill, NJ: Hampton Press 2005), p 196.

48 *Monitoring the Future: A Continuing Study of American Youth*, University of Michigan, 2018.

49 Ibid, 2015.

50 Robert A. Emmons and Robin Stern, "Gratitude as a Psychotherapeutic Intervention," *Journal of Clinical Psychology*, August 2013 Vol: 69 (8) pp 846–855.

51 Ibid.

ACKNOWLEDGMENTS

My good friend, former English teacher John Mickola, patiently edited the earlier drafts of this manuscript. Erik "Pir" Stackhouse provided invaluable tech support and often saved me from pulling out the remaining hair I have left. Lisa Janz gifted my first laptop, giving me flexibility to work on this book from home and my office. Cynthia Halprin-Andreotta, Susan Bailey, Kathy Mottau, and Christine Van Ellis provided ongoing feedback and encouragement.

I am very appreciative of the staff at Global English Editing, as well as MaryAnn Karinch for her time and detailed input that greatly helped me in getting a book contract. I couldn't have asked for a more ideal and productive collaboration than I've had with my talented editor and the rest of the publishing team at TCK Publishing. I've been honored by the trust my many clients have given me and the inspiration I continue to receive from their determination and resilience.

Lastly, I am deeply grateful for my loving family and members of my 12-step program, who help me remember what's truly important in life.

ABOUT THE AUTHOR

Jerry Manney has counselled thousands of individuals and families over the past thirty-five years. He writes numerous articles on family distress, substance abuse, and communicating more effectively, and speaks at national conferences and colleges. Jerry has also taught graduate and undergraduate college courses. While he tries to help each of his clients, each client helps him discover and relearn countless insights. Originally from Passaic, New Jersey, Jerry now lives with his wife in a very small New England town.

CONNECT WITH JERRY MANNEY

Sign up for Jerry's newsletter at
www.jerrymanney.com/newsletter

To find out more information visit his website:
www.jerrymanney.com

BOOK DISCOUNTS AND SPECIAL DEALS

Sign up for free to get discounts and special deals
on our bestselling books at
www.TCKpublishing.com/bookdeals